Opening Yourself

The psychology and yoga of self-liberation

Buddhist Insight, Existential Therapy, Dzogchen

Ken Bradford, PhD

OPENING YOURSELF
The Psychology and Yoga of Self-Liberation
Ken Bradford

Cover photo: Ken Bradford
Author photo: Nelle Engoron
Editing & Design: John Negru

Published by
The Sumeru Press Inc.
Manotick, ON
Canada

ISBN 978-1-896559-78-0 (pbk.).

LIBRARY AND ARCHIVES CANADA CATALOGUING IN PUBLICATION

Title: Opening yourself : the psychology and yoga of self-liberation :
    Buddhist insight, existential therapy, Dzogchen / Ken Bradford, PhD.
Names: Bradford, G. Kenneth, author.
Description: Includes bibliographical references.
Identifiers: Canadiana 20210325844 | ISBN 9781896559780 (softcover)
Subjects: LCSH: Psychotherapy—Religious aspects—Buddhism. | LCSH:
Rdzogs-chen. | LCSH:
    Enlightenment (Buddhism) | LCSH: Existential psychology.
Classification: LCC BQ4570.P76 B73 2021 | DDC 294.3/3615—dc23

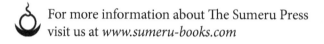 For more information about The Sumeru Press
visit us at *www.sumeru-books.com*

dedicated to

children of earthy wonderment

keen on dispelling confusion and

inclined toward enlightened intent

in being of slightly better help to others

Contents

Preface

THE BONES OF THIS BOOK CAME OUT OF GRADUATE SCHOOL LECTURES I gave on Contemplative-Existential Psychotherapy over the course of twenty-five years. Toward the beginning of this run, I had the high octane privilege of co-teaching with my psychological mentor, James F.T. Bugental. Much of what is in these pages is indebted to Jim's ground-breaking approach to psychotherapy (1978, 1981, 1987 & 1988). He integrated Existential Philosophy, Psychoanalysis and Humanistic Psychology into a practice of depth therapy devoted to the search for authenticity. As I was already familiar with these traditions when I met Jim, I recognized his extraordinary mastery in putting theoretical principles into practice. Combining unremitting empathic resonance with unflinching relational honesty and conversational nimbleness, Jim exercised a remarkable ability to catalyze a person into their authentic presence. Stepping into his slipstream, I expanded his Existential-Humanistic approach by folding in contemplative priorities from Buddhism.

Bugental understood that the potential goals of therapy extended along "a span from helping the client to be more comfortable to a total reconception of the nature of one's identity." (1978, p.2) What Jim understood, even if he did not fully explicate it (thus leaving something for me to do), is that a "total reconception" of the nature of identity extends beyond *any* conception of identity as an independent self existing apart from the totality of existence. It was by virtue of sustained immersion in the full range of Buddhist thought and practice, that I discovered this inconceivable truth for myself. Simply put, the potential of psychological healing extends beyond improved self-understanding to realizing the complete fulfillment (*dzogchen*) of being as such. Conventional therapy goals, valuable though they are and necessary as they may be on a spiritual path, remain in the service, as Chogyal Namkhai Norbu has noted, of "helping one function better in samsara." Whereas, "the Dharma is for helping the individual get out of samsara." (1994, p.13)

This now familiar word, samsara, is important to understand. Literally, it refers to all manner of repetitive compulsions by which we seek to find contentment by filling our sense of inner lack with this or that thing, idea, exciting or tranquil experience, accomplishment or relationship. Samsara is our endless striving for something more or less than what happens to be happening in the moment. As conventionally conceived, Psychology as a field of practice, does not serve Buddhism's more radical goal of ceasing this compulsive runaround and living a life free from *wanting*... anything to remain the same or to be different than it is.

As it happened, my graduate school lectures have undergone a metamorphosis in the writing of this book, coinciding with my leaving academic teaching. This reflects the shift in my life from teaching the art of psychotherapy to more shamelessly delighting and lingering in the mystery of being. Instead of leveraging spiritual thought and practice in the service of psychotherapy, which is what my academic teaching and clinical practice was all about, these pages flip this priority. The goal here is harnessing psychological knowledge and therapeutic praxis in the service of spiritual awakening. Much of the same ground gets covered, but within a decidedly more radical vision of human potential.

Engaging at a relatively young age in contemplative practice and being guided by genuine masters, gave me an advantage in experientially comprehending the theoretical knowledge of Existential philosophers, Buddhist scholars and Transpersonal psychologists. Philosophical or theoretical ideas and experienced understanding of being as such, for instance, are of different orders entirely. This difference is comparable to that between being told what sweet is and tasting sugar for yourself. In being told that sweet is delightful and the opposite of sour, we can form a vague idea about it. But once we actually taste sugar, we go beyond concepts and know sweetness as it is. Discovering Buddha nature, the true nature of the mind, or being as such, works the same way. Like the eye that cannot see itself seeing, the mind cannot conceive itself conceiving. Recognizing the non-conceptual, authentic nature of mind requires opening to non-conceptual experience.

For the taste and savoring of authentic presence, I am indebted to the personal guidance I have received from a number of heart teachers. The short list includes Namkhai Norbu Rinpoche, Tsoknyi Rinpoche, Ruth Denison and Joseph Goldstein. There is no doubt that immersion in the river of wisdom these kind mentors shared with me has influenced how I understand what I am writing about. Occasionally I will quote them, but more often the seeds of their mindstream remain implicit in my words, having been growing in me these many years. Sometimes, when what I say is most clear, what seem to be my thoughts probably began as theirs, so I suppose it is now ours. In turn, if there are insights that resonate with you, which you take in and make your own, your understanding is also ours, even as you, like me, bear full responsibility and freedom for how you live it forward. On this point, any misunderstandings that may have crept into these pages belong solely to me. Also, keep in mind this work, although addressing advanced topics at times, is largely of an introductory nature. For a more precise understanding of certain topics in Buddhist thought and a proper introduction to Dzogchen and nondual teachings in particular, you will need to consult more specific sources and find a qualified teacher to guide you. The same thing is true for Existential therapy and philosophy.

Also, please note that within the contemplative traditions of Buddhism, there are several wonderful words for gnosis, such as *innate intelligence* (Skt. *jnana*, Tib. *ye-shes*) and *awareness as such* (Skt. *vidya*, Tib. *rig-pa*). These elusive words point to the inherently lucid, unfabricated buddhanature of mind. In this vein, I employ several synonyms that point essentially to the same thing. *Authentic, spontaneous, unconditional, instantaneous* and *unfabricated presence* are all more or less synonymous with *nowness, being as such, experience as such*, or simply, *being*. Likewise, the innate intelligence pervading *being* is referred to as *inner sensing*, the *inner guidance system, naked, non-conceptual* or *unconstructed awareness,* and is synonymous with *existential intelligence, self-existing wakefulness, awareness as such*, or simply, *lucidity*. All of these enigmatic words point toward The Mystery. Not this or that mystery, but the inconceivable, all-pervasive mystery of existence.

I am using this potpourri of vocabulary to help launch the conceptual mind beyond itself, by disrupting the compulsive thinking that keeps trying to conceive of what is inconceivable. The point being to not nail things down but to take nails out. So, if shifts in the vocabulary give you pause, perhaps that's to the good if it slows down the cogitating crunch of mind. If the density of my prose or shifts of terminology catch you up, take that moment to be caught up – as in a breeze – and to relax into your felt sense of the ineffable mystery being referred to. Hopefully, this will result in more clarity than confusion. For readers accustomed to Existential philosophy and Buddhist scholarship, which excels in parsing psycho-ontological subtleties, this mix of vocabulary may seem particularly irksome. If this happens, I trust you are familiar enough with this literature to feel irked. So you know enough to consult original Buddhist, Dzogchen or Existential sources that offer more precision. To aid that deeper dive (which I neither encourage nor discourage), in addition to occasional references cited throughout the book, further resources are suggested in an appendix, including selected Dzogchen source texts.

Nevada City, California
under a cold, clear sky
March, 2021

1

Introduction to a Psychology of Self-liberation

Fortunately, some are born with spiritual immune systems that sooner or later give rejection to the illusory worldview grafted upon them from birth through social conditioning. They begin sensing that something is amiss, and start looking for answers. Inner knowledge and anomalous outer experiences show them a side of reality others are oblivious to, and so begins their journey of awakening. Each step of the journey is made by following the heart instead of following the crowd and by choosing knowledge over the veils of ignorance.

— Henri Bergson

The trouble with you is the trouble with me

The prevalent sensation of oneself as a separate ego enclosed in a bag of skin is a hallucination which accords neither with Western science nor with the experimental philosophy-religions of the East. This hallucination underlies the misuses of technology for the violent subjugation of man's natural environment and, consequently, its eventual destruction.

— Alan Watts

As the Grateful Dead sing it, *The trouble with you is the trouble with me, got two good eyes but still don't see.* (Robert Hunter/Jerry Garcia) While this lyric is pregnant with meaning, its essential sense conveys the gist of the human predicament. Even though we are each endowed with an innate capacity for clear seeing, our vision is clouded such that we see the world *as through a glass darkly*, living through distortions and a kind of blindness we mistake for clarity. In this diminished capacity, we find ourselves troubled, making trouble and having trouble with each other, the world as it is, and most troubling of all, with ourselves.

As a civilization, for those with the eyes to see and sensitivity to feel, we live at a perilous moment in history. Accelerating environmental destruction, economic, racial and sexual inequality, psychological distress and its related spiritual malaise are all symptoms of a basic estrangement undermining our otherwise proud, technologically advanced era. However much we try to soothe and distract ourselves from these existential troubles, we cannot long escape an underlying sense of uneasiness that shadows our days and nights. Even though we are reminded that the outrageous violence, including the two world wars, political atrocities, social injustices and genocides of the last century are, statistically, not as bad as humankind's still more barbarous past, the current situation certainly feels fragile. Although more is at stake, globally speaking, than at any time in history, the sense of outer turmoil and inner discord is not unique to our age. Sigmund Freud said that psychological discontent leading to all manner of personal and social trouble is inevitable, being the price exacted by civilization itself in forcing individuals to conform to social norms and mores.

The Buddha presaged Freud's pronouncement in reverse, by observing that the conflicts between self and world, including other people, arise from a core dilemma rooted not in civilization, but in the human psychology that gives rise to civilization. Conflicts between self and world/others are extensions of a more primary conflict within the mind, or self, itself. Recognizing that discontent (*dukkha*) is an indelible characteristic of the human condition, the Buddha observed that all human troubles have a basic cause. This prime cause of existential discontent is what we each have to reckon with in order to have a chance at being liberated from it.

According to Buddhist psychology, the ignorance and brutality of the modern era, as well as all the madness, cruelty and terror of ages past, arise from a fundamental confusion according to which we see ourself and the world through the distorted vision of a mind divided against itself; and hence, the world. That is, we see ourselves and others as beings separate from *being*. This basic estrangement, which we spend our lives trying to overcome, is the singular trouble instigating all other troubles. When we look into virtually any of our aspirations, intentions and activities, we discover that everything we do is devoted to getting us – gradually or quickly – to a place where we are at ease, happy and free in a vital aliveness. However, in striving for happiness, vitality and freedom, we do not see how our efforts are bound, sooner or later, to fail. Not recognizing this basic quandary, we do not clearly see that we do not clearly see. Within a uniquely human opacity, we continually feel an underlying sense of uneasiness and incompleteness which motivates perpetual striving. We do not see that compulsive striving for something else, more or better than whatever is here and now, is the common cause perpetuating our discontent.

Without recognizing the intelligence of existential disquiet – the sense of discontent and incompleteness that leaves us continually *wanting* something more – we live at odds with ourselves, trying to get the outer world to fill our sense of inner lack. Without knowing exactly what it is we are missing or how we have come to feel out of sync, we strive to fill the itchy hole in our soul by becoming the star of our own movie. Since everybody is competing for the same Oscar, we inevitably get into all kinds of rivalries and conflicts and suffer chronic anxieties of inadequacy. Underneath everything, we weirdly feel, as David Loy (1996) has crisply remarked, "there must be something wrong with *me*." Compulsively promoting, defending or sabotaging our self-interests, we pit ourself against others and the world. And since experiences of others and the world are always our own experience, we find ourself pitted against ourself; distant and distancing ourself from the inherent completeness and all-inclusive mystery of being.

These days, the stakes are particularly high. As Tenzin Gyatso, the 14th Dalai Lama, declares,

> What is most pressing, most urgent today,
> is for human beings to become fully human.

Seeing that the outer crises of our age are co-extensive with the inner crisis of self-estrangement, the Dalai Lama understands that in order to better address the world's predicaments, it is necessary to address the inner predicament propelling the outer ones. His understanding is based on the Buddha's realization that we need not be afraid of ourself. On the contrary, he raises an alarm that it is now urgent that human beings become *fully* human, seeing as he does that insanity, cruelty and everyday discontent arise from being only partially human. The fullness of humanity blossoms when we are in accord with our authentic, unpartitioned nature.

This view is informed by two inter-related recognitions: we are not in touch with the fullness of *being*; and it is within our power to be so. The first recognition involves seeing that our identity as a separate, partitioned self is a misrecognition. It is through opening to the pain of separateness that we can awaken the motivation to look into the second recognition, and see the undivided, true nature of our only apparently divided mind. Reckoning with inner dividedness as well as the potentiality for being fully human offers a balanced approach intertwining psychological inquiry and spiritual awakening.

Psychological inquiry focuses on the first recognition, mobilizing self-examination in the service of identifying and loosening divisive and emotionally reactive mindstates. Spiritual awakening congruent with Buddhist priorities focuses on reactive mindstates as well, but aims at seeing through these distortions in the service of recognizing the undivided *nature* of mindstates.

Seeing that both inner and outer conflicts are predicated on a dualistic vision partitioning a perceiving subject from perceived objects, Buddhist psychology understands it is possible to cut off discontent at its root by recognizing its self-constructed, insubstantial nature. While Western Psychology recognizes the projections and introjections characteristic of divided consciousness, it is far less adept in tuning in to the undivided nature of consciousness.

Psyche and spirit

> I think of psychotherapy as an evocation, a calling forth – of the life that is stifled within us, of the inner sensitivity we have learned to suppress, of the possibilities for being which we far too seldom bring into actuality.   – *James F. T. Bugental*

Even though psychotherapy is understood and regulated as a medical specialty distinct from spirituality, the term *therapy* is being adopted by a number of psychological researchers and spiritual teachers to describe the liberating function of the spiritual path. As Paul Ekman, Richard Davidson, Matthieu Ricard and Alan Wallace conclude, "Buddhist practices themselves offer a therapy, not just for the disturbed, but for all who seek to improve the quality of their lives." (2005, p. 62)

Practices of meditation are therapeutic in a way that bears both similarities and differences to the way psychological practices are therapeutic. The major similarity is that both seek to dispel self-illusions and release habitual fixations. Meditation and experience-near therapies likewise de-emphasize theoretical speculation and conceptualizing in favor of experiential inquiry. The major difference between them is that while therapy focuses on untangling the mind's confusion, which it facilitates a liberation from, it does not typically recognize what it is possible to be liberated to. While conventional psychology understands a good deal about insanity and conditioned states of mind, compiling a vast compendium of mental illnesses,[1] it does not well understand the nature of sanity. (Bradford, 2013) Guided by the purpose of awakening to ontological sanity, this book contributes to the Transpersonal conversation devoted to stretching the field of Psychology in this direction.

By the same token, it is now an acceptable if not advisable, standard of care in Psychology to apply contemplative priorities such as empathic attunement, mindful attention and felt sensing to therapeutic inquiry. Harnessing meditative skillful means in the service of healing troubled states of

---

1   Such as appear in the psychiatric nosology of the *DSM: Diagnostic and Statistical Manual of Mental Disorders.*

mind, psychotherapy is devoted to dispersing clouds of delusion and thunderheads of trauma. But psychological purpose does not typically extend beyond emotional repair to the more profound healing that comes with realizing the mind's emotional storms – no matter how severe – are merely passing weather. That is, emotions and thoughts, whether gloomy or bright, are in perpetual motion, impermanent and not as solid as they often seem. It is only when we either fixate on or ignore them that they retain energy and persist as habit formations. While clinical psychology addresses the mind's gloomy troubles, humanistic foci on "positive psychology" and "peak performance" draw upon meditative practices to facilitate brighter potentialities of mind. But whether clinically or optimally-inclined, the focus of Psychology remains on states of mind rather than the inherently free, luminous nature of mindstates.

In failing to address the root cause of discontent, spiritual disciplines justly suspect therapy of missing the key point that allows for true liberation. Certainly, the psychological emphasis on symptom reduction in the service of improving a person's adaptation to a sick society warrants such suspicion. This includes the way mindfulness practices are currently deployed in the service of stress management and social adaptation, rather than in the service of seeing through social charades, the idolatry of the self, and daring a more radical freedom and awakening.

Conversely, psychology is skeptical of religious dogma and spiritual practices that minimize or avoid the gritty personal work of grappling with self-deception. Certainly, there are enough examples of both New Age fluffy spirituality and fundamentalist forms of religious dogma to warrant this suspicion.

On a spiritual path, seekers keen on enlightenment find that a journey into the light goes by way of darkness, traveling on feet of clay. Passing through an emotionally wrenching dark night of the soul once, twice and repeatedly, is not an exception on a vital spiritual path, but the rule. A pilgrim's progress requires coming to terms with increasingly subtle forms of self-importance, self-hatred and self-deception. This requires on-going self-examination. This book thus contributes to the conversation in spiritual circles devoted to integrating psychological sensibilities into paths of awakening. Taken together, the psycho-spiritual challenge is to engage the work and quest of self-reckoning such that spiritual practice does not lose its traction in a flight to light, and psychotherapy does not underestimate the bright potential of becoming fully human.

A venerable Buddhist metaphor depicting the mind as a cloud-covered sky addresses the legitimate concerns of both sides. Like having two good eyes but still not seeing, the image of a cloudy sky conveys how ordinary human vision is obscured. Cloud-covered by compulsive thinking and emotional reactivity, we do not see that everyday preoccupations veil a life-giving sun.

Although it cannot be seen and may only be dimly felt, the sun's illuminating rays and radiant warmth are nonetheless always shining. This metaphor conveys how the luminous clarity and natural compassion of human nature is ceaselessly present even if we momentarily can neither see nor feel it.

Since the light of being always already is (Martin Heidegger), the path of awakening to our radiant nature involves seeing through both everyday certitudes and doubts that obscure the way things actually are. In this view, liberation is not about transcending or escaping the bewilderment of the human condition. It is devoted to honestly facing the persistence of self-limiting hopes and fears. Psychotherapies and spiritual practices informed by this sobriety accept there is a potentiality for being fully human that is unconditioned by the cloud-cover of our social circumstance, family history, racial or sexual identity, and psychological habit patterns.

Confluence of streams

East and West can no longer be kept apart.

– *Goethe*

The three principal streams of knowledge flowing together in these pages: *Existential phenomenology, experience-near psychotherapy,* and *Buddhist psychology* leavened through the contemplative yoga of Dzogchen, share a high degree of complementarity. Each stream respects that the way of healing, or liberating, inner conflicts necessitates opening to the way things actually are, by seeing through the distorted ways we think they are. The process of seeing through obscuring self and world constructs liberates us from those fabrications into the natural freedom and ease of *being*. I have found intertwining these streams offers a comprehensive approach for guiding the work of psychotherapy, including cognitively-based, somatically-keyed, relationally-oriented and energy-sensitive practices; as well as for more capably dissolving the self-deceptions that obscure genuine spiritual awakening. Awakening that is, to the actuality that *I* am not essentially other than you, the world or wonderment as such.

Just as the confluence of mighty rivers makes for a meeting of some turbulence, the conjunction of East and West, philosophy and therapy, and psychological and spiritual work can make for a jostling, if exhilarating, commingling. Even though the initial turbulence in the meeting of diverse streams will eventually settle, becoming a broader, deeper, more powerful river, in the beginning a tolerance for ambiguity is required, involving both intellectual and emotional challenges. In intertwining these streams, this book is really two books. The first part – Outside In – focuses on the psychology of the divided mind in a view integrating Western and Buddhist psychology. The second part – Inside Out – focuses on experientially untangling the divided mind on the way to accessing and resting in its undivided nature.

Since these interlacing streams draw from sources that can be intellectually demanding, I have tried to make difficult concepts as accessible as possible without diluting their radical intent. I suspect that the reason Buddhist, Psychoanalytic and Existential thought strike many of us as difficult is not only that they are intellectually rigorous, but that they call into question our taken-for-granted self and worldview. Turning attention around from its outward focus on objects and ideas withdraws energy deployed in maintaining the subject/object split – which gives us the solid, if illusory, sense we know who we are and where we stand. Intellectually, making this inward turn is difficult enough. But emotionally, it tends to be disruptive in upsetting our taken-for-granted sense of self. Withdrawing energy from external preoccupations weakens the perimeter defenses – projections – through which we maintain a distinct sense of self separate and safe from the wild flux of existence. As our habitual defenses are questioned and become permeable, whatever we have been avoiding (repressing) returns, which may be as disturbing as it is exhilarating and potentially healing. *Healing* not in some fanciful, vague sense, but in its essential sense of being a movement toward wholeness, displaying the natural resilience and evolutionary thrust of a psyche intent on realizing its natural perfection (dzogchen).

The cracks where the light gets in[2]

If the thunder don't get you, then the lightning will.
– *Robert Hunter/Jerry Garcia/Bill Kreutzmann*

Just as sentient beings, ideas and things are conceived, born and develop, everything ages, cracks and dies. One way or another, relationships end, plans don't work out, then do, then don't, money is gained and lost, pride hurt, objects and bodies bruise, break and deteriorate, memory lapses, and the way we think things are keeps turning out to be the way they are not. We seem destined to feel out of control more often than we like and at the mercy of others lacking mercy. Okay, so what else is new? We could fight it, but even though we win a battle or two, we are sure to lose any war against impermanence. So, what if we consider that the cracks in the shell of our self-

2   This subtitle is inspired by a Leonard Cohen lyric.

world are not flaws to be shored-up, but vital openings that let in tendrils of light beyond clouds of self-defensiveness?

What if your life, with all its pain and confusion is no accident, not an arbitrary life sentence occasioned by a meaningless collision of sperm and egg? What if your life is an inconceivably meaningful occasion cosmically tailored for you to more fully awaken from the dream of who you think you are into the The Mystery of who you actually are? What if the wholeness you strive for is already here, just now? Before delving into this most essential of questions, a personal anecdote.

Toward the end of high school, as I was otherwise stumbling through a confused adolescence, a moment of clarity arose as I considered what I'd like to be when I grew up. The outrageous thought arose of my becoming a psychotherapist, and beyond that, a meditation teacher. Mind you, at the time I had no use for psychology or religion of any kind, and was as far away from anything like personal growth as is possible for a dosed and dazed teenager speeding behind the wheel of a tilting Buick. As I fleetingly considered these weird ideas, arising from who knew where?, I found the prospect of psychotherapy flat-out terrifying. Somehow I knew that to go down that road would force me to face hidden hypocrisies I was bent on escaping, and I felt in no way prepared for *that*. As for meditation, I had only the vaguest idea of what that might be. Growing up in a conservative, Protestant family encased in suburban, midwest America, the practice of meditation was the fluffy stuff of exotic fantasy, something the Beatles were oddly, if fascinatingly, into.

Looking back, it is evident that these strange thoughts, completely foreign to me at the time, were not merely idle musings, but were like a meaningful dream or vision. I have since come to respect – perhaps like you? – that such flashes of clarity, as well as darker forebodings of something feeling not quite right, are forms of intelligence it is wise to heed. When an intuition or gut feeling is not distorted by a projection, we may well be in touch with an incisive, subtle perception coming through a crack in our taken-for-granted self-world.

Both in Existential therapy and contemplative practice, it is of paramount importance to discern true intuition from emotional reactions and ideas that might feel right, but turn out to be more projection than perception. Moments of genuine clarity are never contrived, but arrive out of the blue as a kind of grace. In contrast, projections carry with them some tension, or "attitude," that tends toward a hardening of the heart and closing of the mind. You can tell the difference between a perception and a projection by the degree of defensiveness that accompanies it. To the degree there is defensive anger or offensive ambition in an intuition/gut sense, whatever may have once been unconditioned in it has already become distorted by some kind of emotional reaction. Even so, if we become aware of our angry or ambitious reaction, feel it fully and let it be, it will inevitably pass, dissolving back into its unconditioned nature. Like material things, psychic states are impermanent, having no independent, enduring existence. Allowing emotional reactions and mental fixations to dissolve on their own is the essential meaning of *self-liberation*. Understanding why natural release is necessary and how it takes place is the *psychology* of self-liberation. Appreciating that it occurs spontaneously, without effort, is its contemplative *yoga*.

Although inner vision and genuine liberation cannot be willed, the ability to better attune to authentic seeing and being can be developed. Therapy and meditation both helped me differentiate between spontaneous arisings of unconditioned presence and conditioned reactions that seemed right, but upon closer examination turned out to be only me talking to myself. I eventually recognized that being with experience as it is – in both therapy and meditation – is nothing other than opening to the flow of awareness as such. Eventually, I became confident that simply *being* is the indispensable key facilitating all inner work, be it therapeutic understanding or spiritual awakening.

By the time I reached my early 20's, hurled into my adulthood by a personal tragedy I will address later, I was brave enough to bear the self-examination of psychotherapy as well as the rigors of intensive (*vipassana*) meditation. I was also drawn to Tibetan Buddhism, and had the good fortune to meet my root teacher, Chogyal Namkhai Norbu, who introduced me to the yoga of Dzogchen that instantaneously cuts through projections, shattering the carapace of separate selfhood into the spacious vitality of suchness. Concurrently with this, I began graduate studies in Clinical Psychology, leading to a multi-decade career as a psychotherapist. The tapestry of my life evolved as a weave between the warp of therapy, as client, therapist and teacher, and the weft of contemplative practice, as yogi and teacher. The counterpoint between psychological inquiry on the one hand and nondual contemplation on the other served me well in keeping me always a little off-balance. Whenever I was becoming a smug expert in one, the other would come to my rescue, reminding me that the point, as Suzuki Roshi famously taught, was to be always a beginner opening to the freshness of the moment.

Interlacing these streams, this book is directed to those who also have a foot in both worlds, or would like to. Depending on your inclination, you may lean more toward one side or the other. If you are more psychologically-minded, your challenge will be that of opening to and deepening familiarity with the wonder of *being*. If you are more drawn to spirituality, your challenge is to more deeply appreciate that awakening can only be realized through reckoning with the unreleased trauma, emotional compulsions and persistent fixations that obscure your true nature. It turns out to be the cracks in the shell of ego – our embarrassing flaws, desperate hopes, nagging anxieties, secret shames, pathological symptoms, and feelings of inadequacy – that let the light of being in. Although it can definitely be humbling to accept, the warmth of this light has the power to melt defensiveness and aggression that, while functioning to protect us from harm, also sever us from genuine compassion, our innate wholeness and natural well-being. Simply put, the challenge in both depth-oriented therapy and contemplative spirituality is that of opening yourself.

Warming up to authentic presence

I have discovered a nectar-like truth, deep, calm and simple, lucidly awake and without form.   — *Buddha Shakyamuni*

I expect readers will come to this book with varying degrees of familiarity with the notion of authentic presence and experiences of awareness as such. So, for those of you having no direct experience (yet) with being as such/luminous presence/true nature, and for whom these terms sound vaguely suspicious, perhaps like an article of faith I am asking you to believe, I advise you not to believe. At the same time, since you are honestly not sure about it, do not automatically disbelieve either. Respecting your uncertainty, it is best if you adopt a phenomenological attitude, which involves the suspension of both belief and disbelief (which is after all, just another form of belief). Suspend your opinions and appeal directly to your raw experience; respecting your skepticism but without letting it degrade into cynicism. Especially if you are psychologically inclined or a mental health professional, it is also best to read this book in the order the chapters are set out, thinking through the outside-in, psychologically-informed part, before proceeding to the contemplative yoga section. Then, if you are game, apply the exercises[3] in the second part as experiments to test the ideas of the first. These may prove helpful in seeing through the taken-for-granted self-world fabrications lorded over by belief and disbelief. Because, if the Buddha did get it right, and there is a noble purpose and carefree freedom to life beyond being dominated by compulsive striving, it would be a shame to miss out on that.

If you have already had an experience or two of the luminous nature of mind, but have found those glimpses have faded, leaving you with only a vague memory, why not develop your readiness to have more and longer glimpses? To facilitate this, several exercises in the final chapters are devoted to more deeply touching into and gaining confidence in non-conceptual presence.

And for those of you who are well aware of the nondual nature of mind but have occasional lingering doubts about it, wondering for instance,

---

3   Please note the List of Exercises included as an Appendix to locate specific practices.

whether it is this or that state, you might find the last few exercises in particular worth your while. The emphasis there is not only to have more glimpses, but to let the wonderment of being seep deeper in, more thoroughly infiltrating your defenses, saturating your system and dissolving the persistent hopes and fears of separate selfhood. In this vein, if psychology is not particularly your thing and you are already a Dzogchen or other nondual practitioner, you might skip some of the first section and go straight to the yoga of self-liberation.

Finally, for those of you who are well able to drop into and linger in authentic presence, and have picked up this book anyway, I guess your challenge, like mine, is to deepen your trust in innate intelligence all the way to the point where you vanish into it. So for you, I offer what little insight I have as a communion for resting more surely in the vanishing that radiates natural freedom, ease and compassionate vivacity.

As a preparation for actually wading into these waters, the next section is devoted to better understanding the human predicament on the way to better befriending The Mystery.

Part One

Outside In

Understanding the human predicament

pain reassures us of our existence
— Chogyam Trungpa

2

Pitfalls on cushion and couch

Spiritual materialism

Spirituality is cutting through hope and fear as well as being
the sudden discovery of intelligence that goes along with this
process.   — *Chogyam Trungpa*

O N A PATH OF AWAKENING, BLURRING THE DIFFERENCE BETWEEN INNATE
intelligence and the stories we make up about ourselves on that path
can lead to what Trungpa (1973) referred to as spiritual materialism.
This involves the ironic twist of appropriating spiritual ideas and practices
as defenses against the destabilizing – and potentially liberating – effects
of those very ideas and practices. The appropriation is that of taking on an
inflated, spiritualized self-image which functions to strengthen self-importance while avoiding the ego-humbling work of reckoning with ingrained
habits of mind. More subtly still, it refers to mistaking an altered, "spiritual"
state of mind for the unaltered nature of mind. It is predictable that at some
point, whether on a spiritual path or not, we will glimpse the brilliance of
authentic presence, what in Buddhist Sutras is called *tathagatagarbha*: the
womb of suchness. Spontaneously arising experiences of bliss, clarity and
empty-openness reveal the luminous potential of our nature, leaving us awe-
struck. It is also predictable that awe-inspiring glimpses will be fleeting, since
we have not developed the capacity to rest in the groundlessness of open
presence. This being the case, we attempt to create – materialize – a ground
where none exists, thereby obscuring awareness as such.

Since transcendent experiences can be incredible, they tempt us to feel
special in having had them. In the stories we make up about such glimpses,
we may be inclined to identify with these rare moments and strive to have
more of them. Unfortunately, through striving for more "peak experiences," we block our access to genuine openness, and over time are liable to
become irritable, indifferent or cynical because of that. John Welwood was
the first to call this kind of pitfall *spiritual bypassing*, a clinging to spiritual
highs while avoiding emotional lows and internal contradictions. Eventually

becoming disillusioned, we may then blame our self, teacher, meditation practice, those around us, or the spiritual path itself as being deficient; when it is compulsive grasping – spiritual materialism – that is to blame.

But honestly, who does not want to avoid the ego-humbling involved in facing our self-deceptions by clinging to an illusion of self-coolness? It seems to me that spiritual bypassing is an unavoidable pitfall in the process of awakening. Ego's prime mission is to have the upper hand and reassure itself that it is real; preferring to be in the know rather than in the now. To be fully present is to risk being unsupported by the ground(s) of any argument. It is precisely the challenge of being ungrounded and undefended that makes the lightness of being so famously difficult to bear.

Sitting quietly on a meditation cushion poses no real danger, but it does create a fertile space that allows for all sorts of imagined dangers, obsessions and discontent to arise. Which is why it is common on a path of meditation to avoid sitting. But as we persist and discover that meditation is effective in calming our mind and managing stress, we are likely to adopt a regular sitting or yoga practice anyway. As skillful psychic hygiene, a daily meditation practice may well give us a temporary reprieve from our troubled and troubling mind. But if it is left at that, it will only be able to calm the surface agitation of our discontent. This can result in a bypassing where we become comfortably numb. In Buddhism, this seems to especially be a pitfall on the foundational (*Hinayana*) path, which stresses the becalming and renunciation of disturbing emotions.

However, based on the foundational path, a greater path (*Mahayana*) expands the motivation for (and challenge of) practice from focusing on helping ourself to helping others as much as or more than ourself. To the extent we overcome the self-centered pitfall of becalmed aloofness, spiritual practice evolves, becoming more expansive and compassionate. Even so, this altruistic enhancement can also lead to another kind of bypass. Even as self-centeredness is diminished in focusing on the welfare of others, a new trap is sprung if we identify as being a good, helpful person, generous and kind, an attentive listener and so on. This being-a-better-person identity snares us in a dualistic vision that maintains a split between good and bad, blocking access to deeper mystery, freedom and openness. And this is not the worst pitfall.

As contemplative practice continues to mature, a still more dangerous bypass can occur as we become increasingly free and fearless. As deeper holdings release, increased confidence and power flow through us. At this point, which is especially a trap on the Tantric, thunderbolt path (*Vajrayana*), bypassing occurs if we appropriate the high energy of unconditioned presence. To the extent we identify with juicy powers of charismatic magnetism, precognition, telepathy, or of de-repressed righteous rage, avarice or lust, we become possessed by power we think serves us rather than we who serve it. So, how is it best to handle what emerges as we release our holdings?

The historical Buddha can serve as an exemplar whose life shows how to process the radical fullness of experience. Leaving the comfort of his cushy home, he went alone into the wilderness, figuratively and literally, spending seven years rigorously training his mind. After strengthening his capacity for non-distraction (*samadhi*) through yogic practices of renunciation and calming meditation, he hit a wall. Sensing his practice was not working, he stopped striving to improve himself. But rather than merely return to everyday life by going to town and throwing back a few beers, getting laid, building his website, making some bank, and promoting his special yogic brand, he ate a decent meal, sat quietly under a leafy tree, yielding himself to his core question. Something on the order of *What is true?* or *Who am I?* Sitting comfortably and without doing any particular meditation exercise, he opened himself nakedly to the full flux of experience.

Having developed the capacity to abide in a calm presence without obsessively narrating his experience, his repressive barriers naturally collapsed and everything he was holding came up. All his conscious and unconscious desire, hatred, fear, ambition, doubt, paranoia, despair, confusion, you name it. These troublesome states of mind felt to him, as they do to us, like piercing arrows. His openness allowed for a total onslaught: superego attack, id unleashed, ego uncontained, no desperate hope or secret fear held back. It was through this fraught passage that the yogi Siddhartha arrived at the remarkable discovery of his buddhanature. By neither resisting nor grasping what came up, the impaling arrows of aggression, longing and confusion transformed into a gentle

rain of flowers. Not separating himself by so much as a hair's breadth from experience as such, his personal hopes and fears emerged and, like ripened fruit falling from a bough, naturally decomposed into their inherently free, insubstantial nature. Allowing his self shields to drop, the new Buddha made the joyous discovery that existence was unable to either harm or benefit him. Marvelously, being attuned to the mystery of being revealed itself as limitless enjoyment.

Short of such complete liberation, bypassing continues to arise all along the gradient of awakening. Insofar as we are able to access but unable to rest in authentic presence, emotional compulsions, mental fixations and psychic propensities can still captivate us. When this happens, arrows do not turn into flowers but impale us and perhaps those around us, as shafts of suffering. If our energy is low, they impale us immediately; if it is high, they can bounce off our self-satisfied energy shield and injure those around us, returning – in obedience to the law of karma – to impale us later.

Even though the powers (*siddhis*) that emerge through aroused energy and heightened clarity are signs of progress, if we identify with that power or clarity, we slip back into dualistic vision and energize a more potent ego-centricity. When people around us see the high energy of our clarity and charismatic power, they may become spellbound. And if they mirror their sense of our specialness back to us, we are in danger of believing it. If we take it as confirmation of our superiority, we may start thinking we are liberated when we are merely mimicking liberation. This is a condition in which semi-realized persons might abuse their power to seduce, dominate, abandon or otherwise exploit others, perhaps thinking they are exerting a kind of crazy wisdom beyond the consequences of karmic law. (In Tolkien's *Lord of the Rings*, this is like being possessed by a Balrog, addressed in Chapter 15 of this book.) There are abundant examples of contemporary spiritual teachers, including a number of Buddhist masters, who have fallen into this trap.

On whatever level bypassing occurs: becoming attached to a spiritual self-image, a state of calm, identifying as a good person or becoming intoxicated by power, spiritual materialism blocks genuine evolution. The same holds for psychological materialism.

Is normal unhappiness as good as it gets?

I find most people know there is a humbling involved in opening themself, even if and especially if, they deny any such vulnerability. This is a common reason why people delay getting into therapy or, while in therapy, miss sessions or arrive late enough to avoid having to deal with difficult material. It is also why one may quit therapy just when the work touches a core fixation underneath the presenting problem.

Robert[4], for example, entered therapy in late middle age, panicked, sleepless, and on the verge of suicide following the stock market crash of 2008 which threatened to wipe out his real estate fortune. Through several months of therapy, with the unwavering support of his family and the market beginning to recover, his panic subsided along with his suicidal thoughts. This stretch of therapy, his first, forced him to confront the fact that his self-worth

---

4   Not his real name, as is the case with all examples, which may also be composite personalities.

hinged on his net worth. This identification generated a persistent anxiety he managed well enough with material acquisitions, concentrative meditation and frequent golf games up until the crash. An eager and engaged client, he was highly motivated to calm his catastrophizing thoughts and free himself from what he recognized as a "golden noose" of financial wealth. But just at the point where he was able to loosen that yoke, he demurred and left therapy feeling much better. Although I questioned this decision, he observed that therapy successfully addressed his presenting problem, and well, maybe he'd be back to deal with the underlying money issue in the future. So it was no surprise that a couple of years later he left an agitated message on my voice-mail asking for an urgent appointment due to another financial reversal.

Psychological work that conceives of its reach only so far as relieving symptoms or improving social adaptation stops short of addressing the deeper causes of symptoms and innate intelligence at play in those symptoms. A deeper purpose for therapy goes beyond merely feeling better or having a good therapeutic outcome in the lifting of particular symptoms. Underneath symptoms, such as insomnia, an eating disorder, addiction or suicidal thoughts for instance, are the intentions driving those anxious thoughts and desperate behaviors. Attending to underlying motivations makes for the depth in depth psychology.

In the service of becoming more self-accepting, loosening the grip of neurotic entanglements, dysfunctional personality organizations and psychotic panics cannot be understated. It is an indispensable aim of psychological work to address mental confusion and emotional turmoil in order to achieve what Freud understood to be the goal of depth psychology: *transforming neurotic suffering into normal unhappiness*. When therapy goes well and habitual reactions of self-defeating or self-destructive behaviors are loosened, it can literally save a person's life. But much therapy is less a matter of life or death than it is a quest for living a less conflicted life.

Achieving a good therapeutic outcome by transforming a crippling neurosis into satisfying social, sexual and economic functioning, such that one wins a measure of symptom relief and a renewed exuberance for life, remains well within Freud's goal of attaining normal, everyday *un*happiness. To his credit, old Freud was realistic on this point. This is because, even though we go through a vigorous course of therapy, becoming more able to live our own life rather than someone else's, we remain bound by the compulsions of our own life. Even as we reclaim the freedom and power to pursue our own desires and oppose our honest aversions without pretending we are someone we are not, the exercise of that freedom inevitably occurs within a world of others who do not feel as we do. And *they* will dependably disregard and frustrate our wanting in favor of their own. Self-understanding and self-assertion alone will not solve our fundamental problem of feeling anxious, put upon and incomplete.

As it stands, conventional therapy is under no obligation to address a person's deeper existential questions such as the search for meaning and authenticity. But for those who are drawn to realize the deeper purpose of their lives, or who seek a more decisive freedom from anxiety, shame and despair, more far-reaching work is called for.

Psychoanalytic and Existential thought agree with what the Buddha said about suffering, desire and aversion. He observed that it is an existential given we will not always get what we want and will inevitably get what we do not want. Since we normally find ourself *in here*, as a separate, skin-encased entity, we spend our lives in an almost constant struggle striving for and against others and circumstances *out there*. Presuming the existence of an encapsulated, inner self separate from an outer world of others and otherness, we are perpetually dominated by reactions of hope and fear.

Everyday obsessions

The difference between "neurotic" and "healthy" is only that the "healthy" have a socially usual form of neurosis.
— *Norman O. Brown*

Everyday obsessions, known in Buddhist psychology as *worldly concerns*, are those completely normal, "healthy" compulsions driving us to seek security, pleasure, praise, success, personal gain and power, while avoiding insecurity, pain, blame, failure, personal loss and powerlessness. But there is an inescapable downside to the normal, and apparently moral, drives for more and better this and that. Since it is impossible to be sensitive enough to feel the joy of pleasure, praise or rush of power without also being sensitive to the suffering of pain, blame or crush of powerlessness, everyday life is dominated by hope and fear as we struggle for what we want and against what we do not.

The realization of the Buddha is that these everyday struggles are voluntary, even if they seem compulsory. It is possible, as we more fully open to what is actually going on, to recognize our unwitting participation in maintaining the illusion of being a self-thing separate from the world and forever in need of something else. Through considering, and eventually recognizing our collusion in maintaining this illusion, it becomes possible to release it. With a weakening and, in the Buddha's case, a complete cessation, of compulsive grasping and aversion, it becomes feasible to free ourself from everyday obsessions.

Since the striving to have things go our own way is intentional, the suffering of normal unhappiness reveals that this discontent is a form of socially-validated neurosis: an anxiety-mood disorder endemic to consensus reality. For those of us reluctant to capitulate to the idea that the everyday concerns of normal unhappiness are as good as it gets, and who are open to the potentiality of living free from hope and fear, psychological work – whether in therapy or meditation – must serve a non-normative, non-self-centered purpose. Those seeking a deeper sense of well-being and freedom, and who dare inner work to serve that longing, are at risk in conventional therapy of getting sidetracked in a closed loop of self-referencing. Focusing too sharply on a self-improvement project bypasses the basic sanity that is able to liberate a self, whether improved or unimproved.

Psychological materialism

That which we call our "reality" turns out, on closer inspec-
tion, to be our intended meanings, which present themselves
like a dream from nowhere and out of nothing.
                                                    – *Herbert Guenther*

We are also indebted to Trungpa for coining the term psychological materialism. He used this more or less synonymously with its spiritual version. But I find it useful to apply it more specifically to a more essential and stealthy pitfall virtually everyone falls prey to. Whereas in spiritual materialism we overestimate our realization, in psychological materialism we underestimate our potential. This underestimation occurs routinely as we get caught up in everyday obsessions; implicitly in psychotherapy to the extent we identify with our symptoms; and insidiously on spiritual paths when we identify with our shortcomings and sense of incompleteness.

Whether spiritual or psychological, materialism that leads to bypassing refers to the materializing of what is immaterial. This is the process of reification: making solid and real what is transient and imagined. When the fabrication of self and worldviews includes the twist of forgetting that we are the ones fabricating them, this disowning – *ignorance* (*avidya*) in Buddhist psychology – becomes projection proper. Whether we over or underestimate ourself is incidental to the fact we are estimating who we are. Guessing, imagining, hoping, fearing... Construing ourself, others and world involves a lifelong process of bypassing *the now* by living in a narration of what is. This is the common core problem in therapy, meditation, contemplative practice and everyday life.

Narrative bypassing: The story of me

> The more you focus on your sorrows and fears, the more you talk about them, analyze them, identify with them, complain about them, resist them, the more "real" they seem, the more solid and independent of you they appear to be, the more power they seem to have over something separate called "you."
>
> *– Jeff Foster*

Self-examination is invaluable in facing any number of self-deceptions, but dwelling on our past conditioning, current problems and future possibilities, including the prospect of getting enlightened, only reinforces a self-narrative: the perpetually refreshed *story of me*. If it doesn't know where it is ultimately going, self-examination – whether in therapy or meditation – tends to reinforce the illusion of separate selfhood in a narrative that ignores the actual, mysterious, groundless ground of being. As Kirk Schneider (2013) puts it, "The sense of groundlessness leads to great defensive maneuvers to regain ground, or *significance*." (p. 14)

Defensive maneuvers of self-grounding are reified through the stories we hear and tell about ourself. As Galen Strawson discusses it, "*narrative bypassing* [is] living through a conception of one's life or oneself as a 'narrative' in a way that shores up an inauthentic sense of self and sidesteps all sorts of personal, emotional unfinished business, and indeed much of the real matter of life, all in the name of full development of a person." (2016, p. 125) This is especially a pitfall for cognitive and insight-oriented therapies that prioritize making sense of life over more fully living the mystery of it. To be more fully alive requires daring to open ourself to what is not ourself, thereby risking our taken-for-granted sense of self being broken-open in the process.

Since psychotherapy is primarily focused on facilitating self-understanding, its focus is inevitably grounded in self-oriented material. If conceptual understanding is privileged at the expense of felt knowing, insight will remain on a conceptual level. Of course, for many this is of little consequence. Certainly, it is enough for many people to better understand the reasons behind their confusion and suffering. Even better, coming to a clearer understanding helps us be less fixated, as was Robert. But this psychological victory does not mean that we have come to terms with more subtle anxieties, underlying self-doubts and despairing moods. And it most certainly does not mean we have gone beyond the suffering that comes with being dominated by hope and fear.

The signature feature of narrative bypassing is that naked awareness remains bound in the husks of conceptual thinking. That this state of affairs

– thinking that *I* am my thoughts and opinions – is considered to be completely normal, makes it all that more difficult to see that *I* am an insubstantial, fluid, mental-emotional construction project. While the attainment of self and world mastery through constructing an adaptive self-world narrative is a necessary and invaluable accomplishment, it comes with an asterisk.

The victory of social adaptation, with its lifelong struggle of defending and promoting a sense of self separate from the world, ordinarily occurs without our recognizing the innate intelligence that allows this adaptation to happen in the first place. Without seeing that our compulsive thinking dominated by everyday obsessions is not a given, but an aberration (even if everyone is doing it), the most we can hope for is to struggle endlessly for normal unhappiness. Martin Heidegger (1962/1927) observed this entrancement in consensus reality as the *everydayness* of inauthentic selfhood. As he said, finding ourself in socially-validated projections, we lose ourself in the anonymity of *the they*, becoming a *theyself*.

In the service of psychological insight, remaining on a conceptual level of self-understanding spares client, therapist and spiritual seeker alike from the more disturbing challenge of opening to the non-reified – unreal – nature of things. Annie Dillard challenges such self-absorption declaring, "It is so self-conscious, so apparently moral, simply to step aside from the gaps where the creeks and winds pour down, saying, I never merited this grace, quite rightly, and then to sulk along the rest of your days on the edge of rage." (1974, p.276) While psychological work focuses on the problematic cracks in our psyche, narrative bypassing occurs by under-regarding or disregarding the light that streams in through those cracks. Although everyday slang speaks of being psychologically broken-open as being cracked, we need not be frightened by this broken-openness in the way *the they*, conventional psychology, and institutionalized religion often are.

Psychotherapy and spiritual direction defer depth when they hasten to close a crack by applying a plaster of cognitive containment (including dogmatic religious belief) without also strengthening a person's capacity for befriending broken-openness. Becoming fully human necessitates seeing that suffering is not caused by the cracks in the shell of ego, but by the ego-shell itself. Recognizing that a self-narrative has become stifling by its failure to allow us to more fully show up in the world, allows us to consider opening more deeply to that fullness.

Still, the defensive shell of self-narration need not be made into an enemy. A serviceable *story of me* and capabilities of self-mastery are vital developmental accomplishments. Bugental referred to adaptive self-world constructs as our personal space suit that allows us to survive the unimaginable vastness of space. Cracks appear when the protective self-shell of our space suit becomes too restricting. He felt the value of therapy was in retailoring our space suit to accommodate an ever-expanding/growing sense of self.

However, Jim's therapeutic understanding did not go so far as imagining that a self-suit could be entirely dispensed with.

Contrary to this reasonable psychological view, the Buddha found that beyond the limited protection of a self-suit lies a far greater protection allowing for a more resilient and carefree way of being in space. Although it may be a victory to expand a suffocating sense of self into a more supple way of being, enabling us to breath easier and move more freely in the world, this is not yet the game-changing discovery that the atmosphere outside our self-suit is the same as the atmosphere inside. Seeing there is nothing to fear in either life or death becomes evident once we see that we are not separate – and do not need protection – from the otherness of the world.

3

Authentic presence

The mystery of life is not a problem to be solved, but a reality
to be experienced.   – *Alan Watts*

VENTUALLY, I HAD TO ADMIT THAT IN SPITE OF THE FACT THAT THE VIEWS,
practices and goals of psychological and spiritual work differ, my immersion in therapy and meditation over a number of years made it
impossible for me to separate the beneficial effects of each that were showing up in my personal life and professional practice. The calming power of meditation in conjunction with the penetrating inquiry of therapy
leavened by the naked awareness of non-conceptual contemplation, was
seeping ever deeper into my mindstream. Slowly but surely infiltrating
my defenses, undoing persistent fixations, and creating an opening in
which I could not tell where the loosening due to meditation, therapy, my
intimate relationships or my teachers' grace began or ended. It all seemed
to be working together.

Even as my therapy practice focused on the noisier confusions and traumatic tragedies my clients brought in, I found myself working with these
rambunctious issues from within an increasingly contemplative co-pres-
ence. It eventually became obvious, both to my more perceptive clients and
me, that my risking being more unconditionally present with them exerted
a gravitational pull that influenced their own awareness in that direction.
Through repeated exchanges with many clients over a number of years,
a disarmingly simple truth emerged, dissolving wickets of self-doubt and
confirming for me what both Norbu Rinpoche and Jim Bugental had been
teaching in their own ways. What is indispensable to spiritual liberation
and the essential healing ingredient in psychotherapy is *authentic presence:
the capacity of being unconditionally open and unhesitatingly responsive to
whatever is.*

Dimensions of self-liberation

> Man's flight from the mystery toward what is readily available,
> onward from one current thing to the next, passing the mystery
> by – this is *erring*.   – *Martin Heidegger*

In depth-oriented work, deepening the capacity *to simply be* is the royal road to liberation, because being/awareness as such is both the key practice and ultimate goal toward which self-liberation tends. Hence, self-liberation should be understood in three senses: outer, inner, and innermost.

In its outer sense, self-liberation means the liberation *of a self* that is somehow physically, socially, psychologically or spiritually oppressed by worldly circumstances. Outer liberation results in increased *existential freedom* to do as one wishes in the world. In general, the pursuit of existential freedoms is very popular. Everybody extols their virtues and finds nobility in fighting and dying for them. But these popular freedoms we seek and are willing to fight for are external. We want to be free to say, do and have what we want to say, do and have when we want to say, do and have it. Outer forms of liberation allow us to exercise personal freedoms of doing.

In contrast, the inner sense of self-liberation refers to liberation *from a self* bound as a *theyself* living – inauthentically – in conformity to the shoulds and should-nots of *the they*. Emancipating ourself from the dictates of others, including our internalized version of what we think makes us a good or bad person, is an inner liberation that results in enhanced *psychological freedom*.

Inner freedom is not dependent on our degree of outer freedom, hence it is both deeper and more far-reaching. It is quite possible to be imprisoned or enslaved or otherwise a victim of circumstances lacking external freedom, yet still be free in our mind. We are always free to choose how we respond to our captivity, enslavement or other existential predicament. The inner exercise of freedom requires a willingness to accept our situation for what it is, especially if it is impossible or futile to change it. Rather than focusing on externals, this involves changing our attitude toward whatever is happening. The difference between inner acceptance and the struggle for external change is aptly captured in the famous Serenity Prayer: Grant me the courage to change the things I can change, the serenity to accept the things I cannot, and the wisdom to know the difference.

The exercise of inner, psychological freedom demands that we see through the projections of our hopes and fears, daring to be less defended in the situation we are in. Accepting our vulnerability and helplessness certainly requires serenity. But it also presents us with a moral challenge of courage in which we exercise our will to stand up for what we sense is right and live according to our deeper values. Integral to the freedom of inner sensing is liberating ourself from the *theyself* of our own mind. Psychological freedom deepens further as we continue to open ourself, becoming increasingly free of compulsive thinking and emotional reactivity. In this way, we pass through freedoms of doing – whether outer or inner – into the freedom of *being*.

In this third, innermost sense, self-liberation is liberation that occurs *by itself* (*rangdrol*), effortlessly. This is liberation that recognizes there is no self that needs liberating. Innermost freedom is dependent neither on external circumstances nor on psychological maturity or the exercise of moral values. In being essential to human nature, innermost freedom is beyond – foundational to – all physical and psychological conditions. Because it is wholly beyond – essential to – concept and form, it is secret in the sense that the mystery of being is unfathomable, yet everywhere apparent. Innermost liberation occurs, when it does occur, as a natural expression of the innate plasticity, or resilience, of being. Norbu Rinpoche described Dzogchen in just this way, as the Path of Self-liberation.

Gradual and non-gradual integration

> We humans are fragmented and divided beings, at odds with ourselves and our surrounding world. We yearn for a wholeness whose presence we somehow sense as the driving force in our quest for its recovery. — *Herbert Guenther*

In contrast to the rigid dualistic assumptions of empiricist science, which severs observer from observed, the integrative approach presented here is based on a premise of wholeness. Still, the wholesomeness of authentic presence can be approached either gradually or non-gradually.

Whether in therapy or meditation, the most common approach by far is gradual. In gradual, step by step approaches, terms such as *integrative*, *integral* or *holistic* are understood less as a premise than an outcome. In this way of thinking, an integrative point of view is one inclusive of various reference systems, such as East and West, psychology and spirituality, Christianity and Buddhism, meditation and yoga, body, mind and spirit, Cognitive and Behavioral, Existential and Humanistic. In these senses, integration is based on an assumption of separateness, and is accomplished by combining different theories, practices or dimensions of experience into an inter-related whole. Integration is thus an inclusive gathering, amounting to the sum of its parts. Ken Wilber's Integral Theory is probably the premiere example of this accumulative kind of integrative thinking. But it is far from alone.

All forms of developmental psychology and formulations of stages on a spiritual path conceive of growth, maturation and liberation as a graduated progression leading to a more inclusive wholeness. Obviously, any type of development proceeds from an embryonic state of immaturity, ignorance or deficiency, toward greater maturity, understanding and sufficiency. Starting from a beginning (base), proceeding through a growth process (path) and arriving at a fruition makes sense, since we normally see everything as existing in linear time governed by the law of cause and effect. However, innermost, effortless liberation transcends this law.

Liberation conceived as a goal to be achieved sometime in the future collapses in the actuality of its suddenly, and perhaps unexpectedly, occurring. In being authentically present, we find there is no place to stand outside *now* from which to measure before or after, cause or effect. Which is to say, that in a moment of innermost liberation, a seeker discovers that seeking is not other than the sought, the perceiver being not other than the perceived. The great value of a gradual vision and progressive integrative approach is to prepare a constricted, fearful mind for the shock of its breakdown that morphs into a non-gradual – instantaneous – breakthrough.

Since it is common for holistic theories to envision human being in an additive way: mind + body + spirit = a whole person, it is important to respect, insofar as separate aspects are first posited which then need to be integrated, that gradual approaches remain provisional to the actuality of integration.

A more robust integrative approach is based in lived actuality. It proceeds directly as an opening to *nowness*: the non-gradual, instantaneous recognition of wholeness. In fact, this approach is not an approach at all, since it is always already an arrival. Rather than following a developmental, conceptually-designed path, non-gradual paths are poetic and intuitive, based not on progression but instant presence. This is not a way that first divides and then combines elements, but from the beginning recognizes that awareness is undivided in its intrinsic wakefulness.

Non-gradual approaches are implicitly preferred by Existential philosophers such as Heidegger, Maurice Merleau-Ponty and Martin Buber, who seek to turn reifying tendencies on their head, by undercutting the subject/object split and emphasizing the interrelatedness of things. And of course, this is the nondualistic approach favored by contemplative traditions such as Taoism, Zen, Gnosticism, Advaita Vedanta, Kashmiri Shaivism and Dzogchen. Nevertheless, I have found it useful for those of us who are not prepared to open ourself *just now!* and nakedly drop our self-shields, to approach the non-gradual actuality of liberation by way of a graduated path that offers a handrail for more gently opening-up to groundlessness.

4

Divided consciousness: Being of two minds

Two kinds of intelligence

There are two kinds of intelligence:
one acquired, as a child in school memorizes facts and concepts
from books and from what the teacher says,
collecting information from the traditional sciences
as well as from the new sciences.

There is another kind of intelligence, one
already completed and preserved inside you.
A spring overflowing its springbox. A freshness
In the center of the chest.
This second knowing is a fountainhead
From within you, moving out.

— Jalal al-Din Rumi[5]

RESPECTING THAT AUTHENTIC PRESENCE IS THE UNFABRICATED, INHER-ently resilient nature of the mind, allows us to shift the focus of inner work from trying to improve ourselves (and others) to opening to the wholeness which we (and they) already are. In order to distinguish the mirror-like nature of mind from mental fabrications appearing in that mirror, we can begin by considering the two kinds of intelligence that inform these respective ways of knowing and being in the world.

The distinction between objectivizing outer knowing and subjective indwelling intelligence is drawn poetically by Rumi and echoed by Heidegger as he differentiates between *calculative* and *meditative thinking*. Both the 13th Century mystic and 20th century philosopher observe the (ontological) difference between conceptual and non-conceptual ways of knowing. They are by no means alone in making this pivotal observation. Just as spiritual and

---

5   Translated by Coleman Barks and John Moyne, *The Essential Rumi*, 1995, p.178.

psychological bypassing are narrative forms of self and world construction, all constructed – partial – self-worldviews are mental fabrications "acquired, as a child in school memorizes facts and concepts." Recognizing this, we have to face the fact that it is impossible to think our way out of conceptual thinking. To free ourselves from fabricated cages, meditative "thinking" is required.

To the extent we remain in servitude to an objectifying eye, knowing is captivated by conceptual thinking, reinforcing a subject/object split. As mentioned, the severity of this dualistic vision in our world has authorized the de-sacralization of nature, increased economic and social inequality, and exacerbating estrangement from the fecund mystery of being. This outward-keyed, calculating vision reflects Rumi's first kind of intelligence on steroids.

> The conceptual mind is extremely powerful.
> It runs the whole show of samsara.
> – *Chogyam Trungpa*

Heidegger observes that calculative thinking is time-bound, preoccupied with what did or did not happen in the past and what might or might not happen in an imagined future. Buddhist psychology is in accord with this, noting that this everyday way of thinking is how we remain ignorant of the *now*. As Heidegger (1966/1959) put it, "Calculative thinking computes. It…races from one prospect to the next, never stops, never collects itself." One thought leads to another leads to another and another, with the thinker becoming captivated in conceptual proliferation. Unable to step out of the mental churn for very long, a thinker inevitably identifies with their thoughts, losing touch with the unfabricated intelligence that is doing the thinking. Ruminating and conspiring for or against something or someone (including oneself) is the signature feature of a divided mind bound to a "one-track course of ideas." If left unchecked, compulsive thinking becomes a habit that turns into a rut. The more energy we give to mental proliferation, the more concepts become reified and the more our projections bounce back on us. Mentally going round and round, we drive ourself to feel increasingly angry, depressed, euphoric or anxious, depending on what is on our mind; convinced that what we are thinking *in here* is real *out there*. Left more seriously unchecked, this compulsive runaround can get out of hand to the point where the thinking of thoughts solidify into the hearing of voices.

Like a flashlight, calculative thinking has a narrow focus, even as it bounces chaotically from this to that. Concept-bound tunnel vision leaves the felt complexity and wholeness of experience shrouded outside the slender beam of it's focus. Looking outwardly, conceptual thinking feeds its projections while ignoring the projector. Again, both Buddhist and radical Existential thought contend that what appears as a perceived world separate from the perceiver of that world is an illusory construct. Following Heidegger, George Atwood and Robert Stolorow, state this clearly.

> In the absence of reflection, a person is unaware of his role as a constitutive subject in elaborating his personal reality. The world in which he lives and moves presents itself as though it were something independently and objectively real. The patterning and thematizing of events that uniquely characterize his personal reality are thus seen as if they were properties of those events rather than products of his own subjective interpretations and constructions. (1984, p.36)

This fundamental misunderstanding reflects the operation of divided consciousness and the confusion endemic to dualistic vision.

Even though we may be dominated by everyday compulsive thinking, at any moment it is also possible to become aware of our confusion and entrapment in it. This can occur quite quickly, even effortlessly, when we shift from a conceptual run-around to meditative awareness. As Heidegger puts it, "Meditative thinking demands of us not to cling one-sidedly to a single idea, nor to run down a one-track course of ideas. Meditative thinking demands of us that we engage ourselves with what at first sight does not go together at all." (1966/1959, p.53) Meditative thinking is open-ended knowing allowing for mixed feelings and inner complexities to co-exist. This both/and way of thinking turns out to be facilitative of humility, compassion, joy and a sense of awe. In contrast, concept-bound thinking reduces inner complexities to either/or simplifications preoccupied with dividing this from that. "Calculative thinking is not meditative thinking, not thinking which contemplates the meaning that reigns in everything that is." (p.46) Although Heidegger spoke of meditative knowing as a kind of "thinking," he means this in the sense of contemplative awareness. But since we commonly understand thinking as strictly conceptual, it is necessary to clarify that meditative thinking is a kind of non-thinking. It is certainly not closed-mindedness, stupidity or intellectual dullness, but a non-conceptual cognizance that is of the nature of open awareness. This reflects Rumi's second kind of intelligence.

Both of these seers appreciate that of the two kinds of intelligence, non-conceptual intelligence is primary. As Heidegger puts it, "man is a thinking, that is, a meditating being." (p.47) Trungpa expands on this.

> Sometimes, when we perceive the world, we perceive without language. We perceive spontaneously, with a prelanguage system. But sometimes when we view the world, first we think a

word and then we perceive. In other words, the first instance is directly feeling or perceiving the universe; the second is talking ourselves into seeing our universe. So either you look and see beyond language – as first perception – or you see the world through the filter of your thoughts, by talking to yourself. (1984/1978, p.53)

As meditating beings, we are in the world *au natural*, quite literally *with it*. Once cogitating, anticipating and making sense of our situation begins, our inherently open awareness becomes eclipsed by conceptual overlays. This to be expected, since we exhilarate in the rush of power that accompanies naming things and putting things and people "in their place." But as Lao Tzu famously declared, the Tao that can be named is not the true Tao. The true Tao is the Way that is in accord with the flux of experience, undistorted by mental constructs that freeze the dynamism of what is unfolding into something fixed. Attuning to the way things naturally are rather than how we contrive them occurs in a contemplative communion, arising as "a freshness in the center of the chest."

Well aware of the power of mental constructs to cloud our vision, William Blake famously opined, "If the doors of perception were cleansed everything would appear as it is, infinite. For man has closed himself up, till he sees all things through narrow chinks in his cavern." Encased in the echo chamber of mental proliferation, we are bound in a narrative shell. But in attuning to experience *as it is*, Heidegger further observes that meditative awareness functions as "...an opening of man to something, ...an openness. What then, we may ask, does man open to? In a word, of course, the answer is: the given.... [which] too, is an openness and...an opening. Meditative thinking characterizes man's true nature, his being, as openness." (1966/1959, p.28)

While conceptual thinking functions as a deployment of will, meditative thinking is a non-intentional "abiding that rests in itself." (p.66) A *waiting upon* the happening we already are part of. Free from anticipation and settled in itself, meditative awareness reveals itself to be openness as such, functioning without premeditation as *non-action* (*wu wei* in Taoism). The spontaneous freedom of natural resilience is what Heidegger refers to as *releasement* (*gelassenheit*) and Dzogchen understands as *natural release* (*rangdrol*), or self-liberation. As we will discuss in more detail later, non-conceptual awareness is the peerless sword that cuts through all narratives; and in opening to existence as it is, dissolves confusion at its root.

I cannot but smile that in the 13th century, Rumi spoke of collecting information from the "new" sciences. Middle Ages' cutting edge science: what is that? We tend to think that the newest science is always the best and truest word on things, and place great confidence in new scientific knowledge and the technology it spawns. These days, we embrace the knowledge of neuroscience and biochemistry, enthusiastically applying them to the treatment of mental illness. Just as we would have, had we lived in the Middle Ages, embraced the cutting-edge science of the time and applied the innovative treatment of trephining to treat madness. Trephining is the drilling of holes in the skull to release the evil spirits "known" to cause madness. Today, we treat mental disorders which are "known" to be caused by biochemical imbalances, often with powerful pharmaceuticals and sometimes electro-convulsive therapy. These treatments are also innovative and based on cutting-edge science. But today, we look back on trephining with a cringe and air of superiority, seeing it as a savage, misguided treatment based on a primitive worldview and bad science. So we may wonder, what will human beings eight or nine centuries hence, in the 30th century, think about our current psychiatric science?

In our early 21st century, which is super technocentric, dominated by capitalist values still governed by the Protestant work ethic, activities of human doing are highly privileged. Although these priorities are being robustly challenged, the cultural value of being still and doing nothing productive is not as highly regarded. The delicate rustling of leaves along a pavement, the way a shaft of light falls across a table, the sparkle in our friend's eye, the sense of well-being that comes from feeling sated after a decent meal, and the delight in watching a butterfly alight from a flower, do not accomplish anything. Nevertheless, isn't the ease and wonder of these moments – inherently meditative – the goal of all our calculating and striving? We make so many sacrifices and go through all kinds of strife in order to feel more alive and be more comfortable and secure financially, relationally, socially and politically. We so often strive to get to the weekend, vacation, a better world, or retirement, where we hope to finally relax, be happy and free. Our tragedy is that in the pursuit of getting there, we risk missing what is and always has been here. Unable to rest in the overflowing enoughness of things as they are, we think ourselves out of the here and now into the there and then, either a step ahead or a step behind ourself.

Respecting inner quandaries

> The irony of man's condition is that the deepest need is to be free of the anxiety of death and annihilation; but it is life itself which awakens it, and so, we must shrink from being fully alive.
>
> – *Ernest Becker*

Accessing intelligence that is fluid rather than fixating requires that we attune to that fluid fount. This begins with slowing down the speed of our monkey mind. Once we have collected ourself, we are able to listen-in and discover how we are (mis-)construing reality. Only then can we de-construct our self-limitations and tune-in to the freedom we essentially are. Privileging listening-in is a threshold we must cross in order to empower meditative lucidity. As Heidegger understands, "meditative thinking does not just happen by itself any more than does calculative thinking. At times it requires a greater effort. It demands more practice. It is in need of even more delicate care than any other genuine craft." (p.46 & 47)

It is easy enough to talk to or at ourself, thinking about what we ought or ought not do. It is another thing to live the sound advice we give ourself forward. It seems to me we already know in our heart how we would like to show up in the world. But we seem to be of two minds on this. The preoccupied, everyday calculating mind tends to overpower the felt intelligence of our inner compass. As Carl Gauss, the mathematician who discovered the probability curve, is to have said, "I have had my answers for some time now. The only question is how I will arrive at them."

In order to more effectively listen-in and negotiate inner quandaries, it is necessary to respect all sides of our ambivalences and mixed feelings. To become fully human, we have to accept that we both want and do not want to be free. It is not enough to have a good intention and impose a self-improvement program on ourself. This kind of project only works to a limited degree, because the project itself perpetuates an inner split that goes down a one-track course of ideas, pitting a "good me" wanting to change against a "bad me" resisting change. In order to reconcile mixed feelings and dissolve inner splits we have to embrace both sides.

Me and my father

I was terrified of my father most of my life. Having been emotionally menaced and at times physically abused by a man who could be unpredictably "set off," I learned to adopt an attitude of emotional reserve well before I learned anything about the clinical practice of neutrality. This defense strategy served me well in being a good listener, especially when I came to the point of being paid for it. Of course, the price of my self-control also involved the repression of fear and rage. This stemmed both from taking in the model of intimate aggression I learned at my father's knee and the helplessness I felt on the receiving end of his madness. As an adolescent, I found a viable way of rebelling – and securing a degree of self-respect – by alternating emotional withdrawal with intellectually-weaponized political argumentation. Fierce arguments between his right-wing views and my left-ist politics provided inexhaustible fuel for relational bonfires, leaving us both intimately ravaged and emotionally invigorated.

Unfortunately, to the extent this hostile kind of exchange is an element in the way we learn to be intimate, it does not bode well for forming vulnerable relationships down the road. Fortunately, my kind mother provided a hearty counterpoint enabling a wholesome and gentle relational alternative for me to emulate and live forward.

After a number of years of personal therapy and still more of meditation, I was able to buffer the grudge I held against my father such that my reactive mind became less of an irritant, both to myself and those within my emotional blast radius. As it happened, while I was raising my own children, I would regularly host my parents during yearly holiday visits to our home. During these visits, my father and I would occasionally get into political arguments. As the kids left home and I aged into my 50's, even though I had done a lot of work whittling down my "father complex," I was still not free of it.

A day came late one summer as I began to think about the upcoming Christmas visit. That day I hit a wall I could neither ignore nor get around. For days my stomach was in knots and I was miserable just considering the impending visit, even though it was almost five months away. I found I could no longer go on as I had been. After decades of going along to get along, of not being completely honest about my feelings so as to not provoke my dad and jeopardize our family cohesion, I came to a crisis where I felt I could no longer pretend things were good enough between us. And it was obvious that trying to work out my feelings toward him arguing about politics was an abject failure. I felt I had no choice but to come clean and reveal the painful truth about who he was for me. I knew he nourished the idea he was basically a good father with only minor flaws, and that my destroying this illusion would be hard on him.

Over a series of phone and email exchanges during which he resisted hearing what I had to say, I felt forced to tell him that in the dictionary of my life, under the word "terrorist," there was a picture of him. The "war on terrorism" was a dominant meme in the U.S. at the time. I felt his hearing this might actually do him in, as he was around 80 years old and not in the best of health. Putting Buddhist and Christian mores aside, and aligning myself with my best inner sense, I plunged in anyway. Although he initially balked, I persisted and eventually he heard me: leaf, branch and root. As my mother told me a couple of weeks later, she was now living with "a broken old man." This only confirmed that he did, in fact, get it. I could not but admire the moral courage he mustered in taking this bitter truth to heart. And indeed, the depth of his love for me was revealed in his willingness to put his ego aside and meet me shields down. On my side, after I came clean, I felt a dark burden I had carried for many years lift almost immediately. Like steam dissipating in air, my festering resentment vanished, as I found I no longer held any durable grievance toward him. In place of the familiar anguish, anger and fear, a light, fresh love bubbled up, catching me up. I found myself thoroughly looking forward to sharing the upcoming holiday with him.

Even after decades of inner work, I had been neither ready nor able to release the full measure of the pain, fury and resentment I harbored toward him. Until I was. As it turned out, that fierce reckoning served as a clearing, both in the psychological sense of being an emotional clearing-out of a moldy. cluttered basement, and in the ontological sense of being a clearing of open presence. The relational space that cleared through this exchange permitted us to have a much closer relationship during the last years of dad's life, culminating in his final two weeks, when I kept vigil on the floor next to his deathbed, me caring for him and him letting himself be cared for by me. As you might imagine, this was a poignant passage of healing for us both.

The basic human predicament

> What can we gain by sailing to the moon if we are not able to cross the abyss that separates us from ourselves?
> — *Thomas Merton*

The basic human predicament, with which any form of depth inquiry must contend, is that even though we want to be happy and free from self-inflicted suffering, we continue to react in ways that perpetuate it. We both want to change and we don't. If it were as simple as our wanting to change old habits, we would just go ahead and do it. But it's not that simple. We bear within ourselves inner contradictions which can harden into self-conflicts that remain deeply rooted and difficult to release even when we are desperate for relief.

The human condition is such that we tend to suffer from inner tensions, including a panoply of unfulfilled longings, persistent fears and nagging despairs that remind us how we have not come to terms with ourself as we are. It happens that we react to situations in ways we later regret, having acted or failed to act in accord with our deeper truth. It is normal to have idealistic ideas about who we think we are and how we would like to be, and to have these fine ideas undermined by less fine knee-jerk reactions that prove to be stronger than our best intentions. This is nothing new. As is said in the Bible, "The good that I would do, I do not; but the evil which I would not, that I do." (Romans 7:19) When we take an honest look at ourself, we find we are in the predicament, as R.D. Laing (1960) poignantly put it, of living as a *divided self.*

While Laing specifically addressed the severe dividedness of psychosis, a broader implication of his thought observes that the divided self is not limited to psychotic conditions, but arises in conjunction with self-consciousness itself. The dualistic vision of the divided self is the root and *modus operandi* of all psychological suffering, be it psychotic, neurotic or perfectly normal. Regardless of the degree of our inner conflicts, psychological healing involves opening up to the *implicit complexity* (Eugene Gendlin) of our inner tensions, so to more fully liberate the confused roots of our malaise.

Recognizing the everyday predicament of divided selfhood, both radical Existential and Buddhist thought recognize – to a lesser or greater extent – the undivided nature of consciousness that is able to both fracture and heal. Both also recognize it is the loss (repression) of the sense of *being* that is the fundamental straying, which leads to everyday inauthenticity (Bradford, 2019), neurotic misery and psychotic bewilderment. Acknowledging this predicament and the deep need we have to recover our lost sense, Gabriel Marcel mused, "I wonder if a psychoanalytical method, deeper and more discerning than any that has evolved until now, would not reveal the morbid effects of the repression of this sense and of the ignoring of this need." (1949, p.1)

Existential intelligence: the sense of *being*

Presence is a precursor to awe, the humility and wonder – or sense of adventure – toward living. And awe is a scaffolding for wisdom.
                                                              – *Kirk Schneider*

In response to Marcel's concern, Bugental developed a psychotherapeutic approach based in attuning to the sense of being, or *existential sense*. As he put it,

Each of us is invisibly crippled. I believe quite literally that each of us is a handicapped person, diminished in vitality and intuiting either acutely or vaguely that our nature holds unrealized potentials.... More fundamental than sight or hearing or touch or smell or taste is our lost sense, the sense of our own being. The lost sense is the inward vision that makes it possible for us to be continually aware of how well our outer experience matches our inner nature. This is the existential sense. (1988/1976, p.2)

In order to tap our unrealized potential, it is necessary to tune in to that potentiality. Jim understood that even though we may have lost touch with the
vitality of innate intelligence, we still sense "either acutely or vaguely" that
our disconnection is not set in stone. In spite of the effectiveness of our self/
space suit, light keeps seeping in.

Howard Gardner, originator of the theory of multiple intelligences, add-
ed to the rational intelligence that is measured by IQ tests other kinds of
smarts such as musical, mathematical and emotional forms of intelligence.
In addition, he thought there could be a foundational cognizance underlying
all these specific smarts, which he referred to as *existential intelligence.* That
the empirically-based research Gardner relies upon seems to have foundered
on the point of explicating this underlying intelligence, comes as no surprise.
The existential sense is not a sense among other senses that can be isolated
and objectively studied. Existential intelligence is sentience-proper. Cognizance as such can never be identified or studied as any phenomenon apart
from the intelligence that seeks to identify and study it. This, the sense of
being, by its very nature is non-dualistic knowing that can only be accessed
from the inside.

To gain more dependable access to the inner sense, it is not necessary that
we change or improve ourself, but nakedly open to ourself as we are. In fact,
as we are able to more dependably see through the self-illusion, exerting any
effort trying to change degrades our already being-in the flow of now. What is
necessary, is for us to open those habitual ways of being that have protectively
sealed us off from the threats and opportunities of life. When we accept that
in order to be more free it is necessary to risk being less secure, we realize that
opening ourself is not folly but the most intelligent thing we can do.

This sensibility awakens two healing responses. The first, is that tending
to the cracks in a claustrophobic ego-shell is nothing to be feared. This empowers the psychological spade work of self-examination: the loosening of
repressive barriers that keep us safe but at the cost of restricting our freedom.
A second response builds on this recognition that we have mistaken a part of
our experience – self-identity – for the whole of our *being.* More deeply tuning in to the open nature of the self/mind clears the way to deeper liberation.

Appreciating that the cracks in our ego-shell are the windows of our soul
allows us to more ably recognize and bear, as Milan Kundera pithily put it,
the otherwise *unbearable lightness of being.* Meeting our experience without
narration and letting it be and move as it will, allows more subtle holdings
to loosen and be released. Less tethered to a self-image, the challenge then
morphs into getting more and more comfortable resting in undefended,
non-grasping authentic presence. In Buddhist psychology, it is our ability to
bear openness (*sunyata*) that empowers us to risk engaging more authentically
in the world.

Dropping our shields of compulsive thinking and opening to basic intelligence reverses the Cartesian edict, "I think, therefore I am" into *I am, therefore I think*. Simply being naturally loosens projections with their divisive, proliferating tensions. To the extent therapy and meditation are practiced with a respect for the free and freeing play of open presence, to that extent do they accord to the sanity of innate wholeness.

But not to get ahead of ourselves, it may be worthwhile to look into how innate intelligence fractures as self-consciousness arises in early childhood. The psychological human birth, as Alice discovers in Wonderland, is like walking through a looking-glass.

5

Through the looking glass: Emergence of divided consciousness

Ah, not to be cut off,
not through the slightest partition
shut out from the law of the stars.
The inner – what is it?
if not intensified sky,
hurled through with birds and deep
with the winds of homecoming.
            – *Rainer Maria Rilke*[6]

As ANNIE DILLARD (1974) WAS SITTING ON A ROCK BY TINKER CREEK, she noticed a beetle had upended itself legs flailing, desperately trying to right itself. Watching this mortal struggle, she realized she bore a relationship to the insect and its predicament. She could, out of revulsion for bugs, for sadistic pleasure or for no reason at all, squash the beetle where it struggled. She could also simply ignore the bug, thinking its plight has nothing to do with her, and let it flail away. Or again, for no personal gain, except perhaps some slight satisfaction, she could flip the beetle over that it might yet live out its life. In those moments, I imagine Dillard recognized her freedom to respond with casual cruelty, cool indifference or selfless kindness. I imagine she also realized that her responsibility to exercise that freedom was inescapable, since doing nothing in this situation – cool indifference – could well be consequential.

To exercise her freedom in the most compassionate way, she first had to collect herself from thinking and feeling apart from the world. She accomplished this much by wandering down to the creek and sitting on a rock. I assume she did so because she either needed to recollect herself from being lost in a *theyself* or wanted to reinvigorate her *being in the world*. The human predicament of living through a self-consciousness divided from the world, thus needing recollection and reinvigoration, emerges in the course of early childhood.

---

6   Quoted in Mitchell, 1989, p.144.

The mirror stage

> Oh hours of childhood, …we take the very young child and
> force it around, so that it sees objects – not the Open, which
> is so deep in animals' faces…. And where we see the future, it
> sees all time and itself within all time, forever healed.
>
> — *Rainier Marie Rilke*

Human infants pass through a developmental stage in the first two years of life marking the birth of a self-consciousness that separates itself from awareness as such. Jacques Lacan (1977/1966) referred to this passage as the mirror stage.

On the heels of biological birth comes a subsequent psychological birth.[7] It is assumed in psychoanalytic research that prior to the birth of self-consciousness, an infant feels itself to be undifferentiated from and co-extensive with its world/mother. But as this sleepiness wakes up, its easy unity can be disrupted. Early on, when its primary caregiver leaves or is otherwise preoccupied, an infant is able to recognize this relational absence, giving rise to an impression of incompleteness which can elicit a panic, resulting in piercing cries. This existential panic is assuaged when a caregiver responds by holding and rocking baby in comforting arms, and perhaps cooing in soothing tones.

The psychological vocabulary used to talk about this calming rapport is "regulation of affect." This techno-terminology evokes an image of hydraulics. I consider this experience-distant language unfortunate, inasmuch as it leads us to think of intimate relatedness as a mechanical function. What a soothing parent is actually doing is not coolly mechanical in the least, but extending felt attunement in a warm, heartfelt way. This occurs as a caregiver opens to and folds a baby's distress into their own mind and body. This emotional envelopment conveys a palpable reassurance that existence is manageable. And that is not all. Such soothing rapport takes place as an emotional exchange that is transacted in a currency of love. Compassionate attunement imparts a direct, non-conceptual impression of completeness to a panicked infant, who feels in that moment existentially incomplete. Providing this refuge facilitates for the baby a basic trust in *being*. I would say this relational sharing is a more fertile way of understanding how "affect regulation" is facilitated.

In addition, since a baby's shrill cries are upsetting to a sensitive caregiver, the soothing of infant distress also works for the caregiver as a measure of self-soothing, helping the adult to also feel things are manageable. In calming an upset baby, a parent simultaneously calms their own empathic

---

7   See Mahler, Pine & Bergman, 1975.

upset. This primal human exchange reveals how *inter-being* is primary to our sense of being a separate being. Perhaps research psychologists prefer the technical terminology because they feel too embarrassed or unscientific to use more experience-near words such as love or compassionate response. Even though that is certainly what is being shared in these moments.

In considering the mirror stage, phenomenologically-keyed child psychologists speculate that an infant's impression of incompleteness is amplified as they witness others displaying abilities which they lack. Since an infant's brain develops faster than its physical coordination, it is aware others can do things that it cannot, like walk on two legs and converse with each other. This lagging of physical ability behind mental development is what Lacan describes as the "specific prematurity of birth". (1977/1966, p.4) He suggests that as an infant sees it is lacking in ability, it is left feeling fragmented and insufficient. This self-awareness evokes a sense of inadequacy that is laid down at the foundation of self-identity. This is why growing beyond a fragmented, deficient sense of self to an intact, able sense of self – through the mirror stage – is a developmental accomplishment accompanied by great pride and joy for a baby. Having a sense of inadequacy at the floor of nascent selfhood at least partially explains why it can be so difficult to work through nagging self-doubts later in life. To dispel our sense of personal inadequacy as an adult challenges us to untether ourself from ourself at the deepest level of our self-image.

Lacan drew upon intriguing primate research in forming the theory of the mirror stage. Research comparing chimpanzees with human infants was conducted to ascertain the point at which the psychological development of chimpanzees and humans diverge. In these studies[8], chimpanzees placed in front of a mirror would notice the image of a chimpanzee in it. Without recognizing the image as their own, the chimpanzees would get excited, approach the mirror and look behind the glass for the chimp they saw. When no chimpanzee was found behind the mirror, they lost interest in the mirror and sought other physical objects to engage. When human infants are presented with the same circumstance, roughly up until one year of age, they behave similarly to the chimps. Seeing an image of a baby, an infant approaches the mirror, looks behind it, and finding nobody there, likewise loses interest in its image.

However, a significant change occurs for human infants around the end of the first year of life, marking a divergence between the species. At that point, upon seeing the image of a baby, a human infant approaches the mirror and without venturing to look behind it, greets its image jubilantly, laughing and exhilarating in self-recognition. The theory holds that up until this point, the baby, having suffered many impressions of incompleteness,

---

8   Reported in Merleau-Ponty, 1964/1960.

now enjoys – vis à vis its self-image – an impression of completeness and perfect capability. In the looking glass, when the baby moves its arm, the mirror image moves its arm just so. Whatever the baby does, the self-image perfectly obeys as the wee one squeals with delight with their newfound power and mastery.

Up until this turning-point, an infant's sense of itself has been located in its body, even as its body-self was felt to be fragmented and frustratingly un-able to do things. Through the mirror stage, an uncoordinated, fragmented sense of self is succeeded by an intact, perfectly able *me* in the mirror. The baby no longer locates itself solely in a physical body, but (literally) finds itself in a mental body. This inaugurates a developmental leap, as the self-entity with which the maturing infant comes to identify takes shape as a fabulous apparition. Fantastically, a self-image becomes more than merely a two-dimensional reflection. Since it seems to reveal the psychic depth of a cohesive, idealized self, imbuing an optical image with emotional heft.

From the mirror stage on, we cannot help but see ourself from the outside in, just as others see us and we see them. This marks the genesis of the split between an imagined me and a felt me. From this point on, *I am an Other* (echo Rimbaud). *I* am affected not only by what happens to my body, but also by what happens to my self-image. It comes to matter a great deal how I am seen and how I see myself: *who* I am. As we know, injured pride often takes longer to heal than a broken bone. As Merleau-Ponty put it,

> At the same time that the image of oneself makes possible the knowledge of oneself, it makes possible a sort of alienation. I am no longer what I felt myself, immediately, to be; I am that image of myself that is offered by the mirror. To use Dr. Lacan's terms, I am 'captured, caught up' by my spatial image. Thereupon I leave the reality of my lived me in order to refer myself constantly to the ideal, fictitious, or imaginary me, of which the specular image is the first outline. (1964/1960, p.136)

Of course, as an imaginative fiction, reified selfhood is not real; but this does not stop us from pretending it is. And of course, a young child does not literally believe it is *in* the mirror-image, but finds itself *vis á vis* an imagining. An infant-toddler locates itself in the reflective space between body and image, but fails to recognize the nature of this in-betweeness (openness/ groundlessness). It is in this sense that the Buddha said self and world exist like a mirage, reflection, echo or rainbow. Existence *is*, but not in the objectivized-reified way we imagine it.

The desire of wanting to be seen, loved and validated feels like an undeniable, primal need. The underlying sense that something is somehow missing, insufficient or wrong with *me,* leads to a lifelong disquiet. Buddhism refers to this as chronic discontent (*dukkha*), and Laing as ontological insecurity. Thus the human paradox: the birth of self-consciousness gives rise to an increased sense of self-cohesion, self-mastery and the impression of having a firm ground under our feet, while simultaneously giving rise to an increased sense of separation and anxious fragility that distances us from the (groundless) ground of being. As Merleau-Ponty summarizes, "childhood makes possible both a development unknown to animality and an insecurity that is proper to the human child. For inevitably there is conflict between the me as I feel myself and the me as I see myself or as others see me." (1964/1960, p.137)

With the advent of more recent animal research, it can no longer be said that this human development is "unknown to animality." It now appears that bottle-nosed dolphins, some primates, magpies and elephants at least, can recognize their images in a mirror. This suggests that what we anthropocentrically think of as a special quality of humanity is actually not human-specific, but a quality of consciousness available to other sentient beings. Even so, it is not apparent that other species' mere ability to recognize their self-image has the same formative meaning in the development of divided consciousness as it does for us.

The term mirror stage arose in a culture that has mirrors. But as a stage of human development, it does not require the existence of glass or metal mirrors, since it can be accomplished by any medium allowing for self-reflection. This could be a still pool. But much more importantly, it could be and always is the eyes of another person. Developmental psychology respects the relationship between parent and child as essential to the formation of a sense of self, healthy or unhealthy. Games of peek-a-boo are widespread transcultural exchanges that belong to the imaginative play of self-consciousness concurrent with and subsequent to the mirror stage. And certainly, of more import than any game or passive self-recognition in a reflective surface, is how a child comes to see itself through the eyes of its primary caregivers.

Contributing to the emotional heft of self-identity, an infant-toddler comes to see itself through being seen. As Laing put it, "The need to be perceived is not, of course, purely a visual affair. It extends to the general need to have one's presence endorsed or confirmed by the other, the need for one's total existence to be recognized; the need, in fact, to be loved." (1960, p. 128) When a baby is held in the arms of a caregiver gazing into that baby's eyes, what does the infant see being seen? How a parent sees a baby is how the baby first comes to see itself. The gaze of the parent serves as a primal mirroring which conveys a great deal of information an infant has no choice but to take in. The gaze could be loving, exhausted, admiring, resentful, indifferent, distracted, happy, depressed, flipping back and forth, et cetera. Whatever a parent's habitual mood and feelings toward themselves, their situation and the infant, the repetition of a habitual state will be what a baby sees in *their* eyes, reflecting *its own* existence. This early empathic exchange forms the ground for the development of a more fleshed-out sense of self to come.

Core vulnerability

> The essence of normality is the refusal of reality.
> — *Ernest Becker*

As a child enters the mirror stage, they are already predisposed to the emotional rapport that has constituted their relational field(s) with their parents and other caregivers. While the early childhood family soup is unique for each of us, the shared emotional driver of self-formation is, as Laing observes, the need, if not demand, to be confirmed and loved. This deep relational *wanting* is humanity's core vulnerability. The partitioning of awareness into self versus other divides us such that we feel vulnerable to and anxious about being disconnected, unloved, unworthy and invisible.

On this point, Laing suggests that self-consciousness is based on the principle *esse=percepi*: to be is to be seen, and *percepi=esse*: to be seen is to be. The need to be seen and confirmed works on two levels. On a mammalian level, it satisfies something in our species-specific nature of belonging to a social group. Deeper down, it is self-validating, reassuring each of us that we separately and independently exist. When this occurs through good-enough parenting, a child is likely to have a secure attachment with others; and I would add, with otherness, whether outside or in. This is facilitated by having been held with care and lovingly seen as a child, empowering both a basic security-trust in being here and conveying the sense that we are also good-enough. This strengthens the ability to better tolerate the self-doubt that invariably accompanies self-consciousness.

According to Laing's formula, to not be seen or loved presents a child with a negative mirroring experience. This failure exacerbates the underlying sense of incompleteness, leading to insecure attachment and increased anxiety that *I* may not exist. Instead of fortifying an illusion of completeness, negative mirroring undermines the sense we *are part of* a larger whole, while inflaming the suspicion we are *apart from* a greater wholeness. This intensifies the sense of separateness, resulting in a more seriously divided self. But wherever we fall along the continuum of having received positive-to-negative mirroring, we cannot escape the fate of *esse=percepi* and the ontological insecurity of this vulnerability.

As a result, at the root of every independent sense of self lies a hidden dependency that makes for a kind of vertigo. This neediness is lived as the compulsion to repeatedly solicit others for confirmation that we are worthy, special and not beyond love. We depend on others to service the illusion of our independence. Many of the personal projects we pursue and virtually all of the social games we play are devoted to confirming an illusion of self-existence. And of course, others are playing the same game with us. Such is the social bargain of *the they*. The pop psych book that made a big splash in the 1960's, *I'm OK, You're OK*, is based on the implicit suspicion I'm not OK, and neither are you. Thinking that security and fulfillment come from the outside to an *I* on the inside, neediness is never satisfied for long and never ends. Although we can anesthetize our sense of *wanting* or try to deny it, we cannot evade it, because it is what defines us.

Transitional experience

Mortals, who among our race
Has given this thought its weight,
That on this passing moment hangs
Our everlasting state[9]

It is common to think that growing up ends when we reach adulthood. Yet it is apparent that maturation can proceed throughout our lifespan as we deal with existential challenges such as serious illness, marriage, divorce, parenthood, midlife, elderhood and death. But these life transitions mark only some highlights in our passage through time. Life in its entirety is a transitional experience open at its ends to the mystery of where we came from and where we are going to.

The pediatrician/psychoanalyst, D.W. Winnicott, noted that throughout the lifespan, children and adults try to smooth the passage and buffer The Mystery by relying on self-grounding supports. He understood that reassuring supports do not exist in themselves, but function as *transitional phenomena*. Among the many possibilities of self-grounding, he famously gave special attention to young children's transitional objects, which overlap with the mirror stage. As we know, it is common for children to adopt a self-soothing object, such as a blanket or stuffed animal, to help negotiate the passage from helpless infancy through toddlerhood to a more autonomous selfhood. It is certainly a developmental achievement when the insecurity evoked in discovering we can be a separable, vulnerable self, can be allayed by having a cuddly, enduring object to hold, fondle and love.

9   As inscribed on the slate tombstone of Capt. Elijah Anderson, 1733-1806, Conway, Massachusetts.

This object relationship is a victory of self-soothing that serves a transitional function, but transitional to where? Such objects are transitional insofar as they are employed until a child matures to the point where they feel secure enough in being a separate self that they no longer need a material crutch. This understanding is central to the psychology of child development that conceives "separation and individuation" to be the goal of growing up.

In addition to a material transitional object, a baby's babbling, thumb-sucking and other forms of auto-eroticism are also recognized as forms of transitional experiencing. Winnicott observed that all these activities occur in "an intermediate area of experience" mediating contact between inside and outside. Through engaging these self-soothing practices, the infant and toddler "play" with a "membrane" (1971, p.2) mediating their inner reality and the outer world. At the point when the membrane is strong enough and *sets*, it is assumed that the developing self has achieved a kind of optimal permeability that is able to modulate existential vulnerability. The child becomes able to be open to the world while moderating that input so as not to be overwhelmed by it. Arriving at this point of self-world mastery, the psychological birth of the infant is considered to be pretty much complete. Having formed an effective ego-skin, it is assumed that the child has passed through the intermediate area Winnicott noted, being psychologically born as a separate, autonomous self.

However, from the more holistic perspective of becoming *fully human*, adequately transitioning from infancy through childhood and adolescence to adulthood, becoming an ever more cohesive, masterful self only means we have constructed a socially-competent divided selfhood.

One of Winnicott's most radical insights into self-development, which has been largely neglected in Psychology, is that human beings never actually make it through transitional space – from infantile insecurity to the solid ground of grown-up security. As he put it, the "intermediate area of experiencing, to which inner reality and external life both contribute...is an area that is...a resting-place for the individual engaged in the perpetual human task of keeping inner and outer reality separate yet interrelated." (p.2) It is not, as we would like to believe, that human life proceeds simply and linearly from undifferentiated chaos to a clear and distinct differentiation between inner and outer, self and other. Looking more deeply into a settled, self-grounded state, we discover it lacks both enduring settledness and dependable groundedness.

We never fully succeed in crossing the abyss of otherness to the ground of authentic selfhood. Imaginatively formed in the in-betweeness of the mirror stage, experience remains transitional, always occurring in an intermediate area, neither absolutely here nor there. This is another way of saying that experience occurs in the space of inter-being, even though an experiencing self fails to recognize its essentially spacious nature. Winnicott's insight, echoing the Buddha, is that while we never leave transitional space, we think we do. We ignore the groundlessness of our transitory nature through the narrative 24/7 feedback loop of self-referencing, constantly reminding ourself we exist. But perpetual self-world construing never succeeds in establishing either a discrete self inside or a secure world outside the stream of consciousness.

Of course, children outgrow their transitional objects. The baby blanket morphs into the command of speech. And through language, we deploy the power of conceptual understanding to participate in the games of the social world. As a clutch of 20th century thinkers have noted, language itself is a transitional phenomenon. With language, we are lured to assume that because a thing can be named, it exists independently as that thing, rather than interdependently in a linguistically fluid, relational matrix.

The ability to exercise our conceptual intelligence in the exercise of our will seems to confirm both our personal power and the solidity of the outer world we are able to manipulate. However, the flaw in this everyday assumption is that language and its consensual constructs remain always unfinished in an evolving process, granting us no true ontological security. We forever exist in transition – always on our way to somewhere – and wherever we arrive, that place is only a temporary stop on our way to somewhere else. Of course, we are free to settle on any temporary campground we like, including the grounds of an argument we hold dear. Or a love affair we hope will "make my life complete, all my dreams fulfill" (Elvis Presley). But since we also know it is possible to lose any of our security arrangements, we suffer the on-going discontent of anxiety, despair and aggression.

The measure of our capacity for genuinely dealing with ontological insecurity is the degree to which we allow for reality-testing. To discover what is real and true, it is necessary to become permeable to that truth. Which means daring to soften our self-world membrane, unzip our self-suit and open to the immensity of being we have developmentally succeeded in mastering; that is, repressing.

Primal repression

[Self-world constructs] form a curtain of fantasy, where everything is clear. It does not worry [the construer] that his "ideas" are not true, he uses them as trenches for the defense of his existence, as scarecrows to frighten away reality.

— *Ortega y Gasset*

The emergence of self-consciousness marks the simultaneous birth of divided selfhood and a personal unconscious. Identifying as *I* casts a long shadow of *not-I*. In considering the origin of the unconscious, Freud posited a primal repression on the basis of which all other repressions occur. Loy expands upon this, suggesting, "perhaps our primal repression is not sexual wishes (as Freud thought) nor fear of death (as many Existential psychologists think) but the quite valid suspicion that *'I' am not real*." (1996, p.*xi*) The mirror stage inaugurates a primal repression through which we locate ourself outside ourself. From this point on, experience for the most part is mediated through a running commentary which maintains the illusion of our being a separate entity.

The good news is that self-reification carries with it a get out of jail free card. Since who we take ourself to be is imaginal, this dreamlike nature means we are not as trapped as we may feel. If the self really was a fixed entity, which Ernesto Spinelli (2019) describes as the "dictatorship of I" rather than the plastic, transitory process it is, we would indeed be in a fix, because change would be impossible.

A case could be made that the art of living involves a process throughout the lifespan of weaving a curtain of fantasy out of the mystery of existence. The jubilation of self-identity during the mirror stage is the beginning of a lifelong challenge to adapt to, excel in, celebrate, invent, articulate, mourn, fight, sing or dance a life. In discussing the birth of theatre in Classical Greece, Nietzsche noted that creative imagining is a way to mediate dread and sorrow. He wrote, "in the supreme jeopardy of will, art, the sorceress expert in healing, approaches him [who is stricken]; only she can turn his fits of nausea into imaginations with which it is possible to live." (Quoted in Bradford, 1989, p.229) Even though the art of living may be nothing more than creative imagining, it is still an adaptive play of illusion creating a habitable self-world.

If this was all that self-consciousness asked of us, it would not be a problem. But since our self-world art-iculations are fundamentally defensive, they cannot heal the basic split that leaves us *wanting*. To heal primal repression, we require not only an art of living, but an art of dying into life. This requires seeing through illusions we mistake for reality.

6

The phantastic self

The range of what we think and do is limited by what we fail
to notice.   – R.D. Laing

TO THE EXTENT WE DO NOT SEE OUR IMAGINATION IS THE ARCHITECT OF A
dreamlike self inhabiting a dreamlike world, we do not recognize the luminosity of our dreamlike nature. Failing to discern the inner illusionist, we
do not notice our reality is marvelously unreal. Adopting a defensive posture,
we avoid testing our reality too thoroughly. The waking dreams of consensus
reality may not be a problem as long as we remain comfortably numb going
along to get along. But by virtue of the nature of divided consciousness which
leaves us perpetually *wanting*, it proves impossible to escape the nagging disquiet of our longing for wholeness. More clearly understanding the emergence of self-consciousness in childhood may help us be more sympathetic to
our human predicament, but it does not address our adult conundrum. How
is it that a phantastic sense of self congeals into a convincing self-illusion?

An obvious way of cutting through the trance of separate selfhood is
by looking directly into our self-sense. So, before considering the Buddhist
psychology of non-self, I invite you to make a personal inquiry. This exercise
can be done either alone or with a partner.

Exercise 1

Who am I?

Solo inquiry: Take a moment to prepare by giving calculative thinking a rest.
Let the thinking mind settle by sitting in a comfortable, upright position,
allowing your spine to come into alignment, your chest and belly to open,
and your breathing to be full and unencumbered. Slowly take three or four
deep breaths, slowly inhaling and exhaling completely, letting your body
relax and energy flow freely. Present and alert in a place of inner stillness, ask,
Who am I?

Note whatever arises as an answer. If you wish, jot it down, perhaps in
a journal, and set it aside. Then freshly ask the question again. Note what

comes up, jot it down and set it aside. Take a moment and another deep breath or two, and repeat the question. Do that again. continue repeating it as long as different answers keep coming. Several self-definitions may arise that are notable, such as your sex, race, family status, occupation, hobbies, et cetera. Patiently note each one until nothing else comes up.

When no more self-definitions arise, and having set aside all that have arisen, notice what is left. That is, since there is nothing left to notice, notice the empty vividness of awareness as such.

Then, without repeating what you have already found, consider, *Who is noticing?* or *Who is asking?* Again, observe what arises, and if something does, ask, *Who knows this?* Continue to look into yourself in this way, asking, with each new something that arises to define you, *Who knows this?* As you proceed, continue to notice the content that arises, and also tune in to the knowing of the knower of all these things. Are you the content that arises or/and are you the knower of that content?

Consider: *Is there a knower apart from the knowing?*

Dyad inquiry: Same as above, except done with a partner who repeatedly poses the simple question, *Who are you?* to the inquirer. And, as appropriate, follows that up with, *Who knows that?* but without adding any further commentary. When the inquirer comes up empty, switch roles. After both partners have inquired, debrief what you have each experienced within the dyad; and then do so in the larger group that may have broken into dyads for the exercise.

Question and answer exchange with a student inquiring into *Who am I?*

Jane: I'm having a hard time with this. OK, I'm open and present. And I find my mind is really busy. If I have an inner world, it is in my mind and ideas, and sometimes these feel like they're pure and mine, but other times they are what I've learned from others. And sometimes I resonate with them, but other times I don't, or I'm not sure what is me, my inner guidance and what is really what I've adopted from teachers or my parents or what I read.

Ken: OK. So who has these ideas…? Who are you?

J: I'm working on defining that.

K: Are you your ideas?

J: I could be.

K: You don't sound convinced.

J: I'm not sure.

K: How is it that you know that you do not know for sure?

J: (laughter) I don't know...and yet I know....

K: It's something of a mystery, isn't it? There is felt awareness that bubbles up; we say "from within." This is key. As we look within and open to our question, some knowing may arise, or it may not. But in either case, we are in a mood of wonderment. For a moment, we are neither for nor against anything, but open to mystery.

J: I get the mystery, but I have a hard time with the no self thing. Why was the Buddha opposed to the self? What does he have against it? Because we identify too much with our story?

K: OK, let's look into that. You have a hard time with this no self thing. Can you put your finger on who has difficulty with this idea? (pause) As you look into the difficulty, is there a self-entity separate from the difficulty itself? What do you find?

J: Ah, ...I do find this upsetting and its unnecessary to kill off the self.

K: Alright. And notice how those are two things. Being upset is the first thing, and then thinking the no self idea is an unnecessary assassination is a further step based on that. Is that right?

J: (assenting with a head nod)

K: You can *feel* the upset. And you also notice the *idea* of no self strikes you as unnecessary. Is that right?

J: (another slight head nod)

K: OK, you have a feeling and an idea. But the question here isn't about your particular idea or feeling, but who is having them. So, can you put a finger on a her who is other than the feeling and idea?

J: I'm coming up empty here.

K: (long pause) How about that? No there there?

J; I don't know.

K: In allowing yourself to honestly ask the question, you are opening yourself to not knowing, which is already an honest display, I would say, of authentic presence. I call your openness authentic, because you are not fabricating anything. You are letting your awareness be as it is: open and wakeful. In looking for a self, you may not find anything, but the non-finding is itself full of sensitivity and awareness, isn't it?

J: Right.

K: (light laughter) Right. Coming up empty and not finding a separate self: Is that a problem?

J: (a smile) Not really.

K: How about that?

J: Its kinda weird. (continued smiling) Makes me a little light-headed.

K: (also smiling) Sure. A little *lightness of being* then?

J: (a slight laugh) Ah ha.

Non-self

He invented a face for himself.
Behind it, he lived, died, and was resurrected many times.
His face today has the wrinkles from that face.
His wrinkles have no face.   – *Octavio Paz*

Under the Bodhi tree, the Buddha recognized three indelible existential characteristics. Along with the pervasiveness of discontent (*dukkha*) and impermanence (*anicca*), he discovered the self doing the recognizing could not be found. Looking into the looker, he discovered that the seemingly real self – *atman* – does not exist as anything more substantial than a mirage, echo, rainbow, or reflection. He saw the self to be no self: *anatman*. (The Sanskrit prefix *an* means non- or no.) In this trio of existential givens, non-self is certainly the most radical, disturbing and staunchly resisted. It is difficult enough to accept that everything in life is impermanent and we are destined to lose everything we love, including life itself. Still more daunting, is facing the truth that all our efforts to secure lasting pleasure, admiration and various kinds of gain, while trying to avoid pain, criticism and all kinds of loss, are bound to fail or at risk of failing; causing us on-going anxiety, irritation and despair. But most disturbing of all is the audacious possibility that *I*, myself may not exist. That dizzying prospect leaves us facing an abyss.

However, when the nature of our self as a non-self is actually experienced by someone prepared to see through the self-illusion, the non-existence of separate selfhood is a liberating recognition. Self-groundlessness discloses itself as ecstatic openness. It becomes apparent that *I* am not my thoughts, emotions or perceptions; neither am *I* other than the thoughts, perceptions and emotions which arise and pass through awareness. Even though a specific self cannot be located, neither can self-awareness be denied. Awareness of this non-finding turns out to be spacious, saturated with clarity and expansive in well-being.

In the absence of clinging to a solid self, we find, as did the Buddha, a blissful lucidity expressing itself as psychic plasticity, which is, ironically, prone to losing itself in the vividness of its own percepts and concepts. Taking perceptions and ideas as real displaces our attention from awareness as such onto the objects perceived and ideas conceived within awareness. Being captivated within a self-world narrative is what Zen means in describing samsara as losing oneself in *the 10,000 things* of phenomenal existence. Taking our self-world construction as real is a psychic illusion which, as noted earlier, must be constantly maintained lest it naturally collapse into the flux of its transient selfless nature.

Importantly, non-self does not mean anything as simplistic or nihilistic as "I don't exist." As Trungpa put it, non-self "does not mean simply the absence of ego itself. It means also the absence of the projections of the ego." (1978, p.7) It is not only that an inner self is not real, but that the self's world does not exist as one thinks it does. The self-illusion is maintained through a constant commentary of self-referencing vis à vis others and otherness. Trungpa observes that the self "maintains its identity by means of its projections. When we are able to see the projections as nonsubstantial, ego becomes transparent accordingly.... Once we have dealt with the projections of ego and seen their transitory and transparent nature, then ego has no reference point." (p.7&8) Being without a reference point allows for the bubble-like nature of ego to pop as the openness of awareness expands.

Since at least the Renaissance, individual selfhood has formed a basic building block of society, authorizing the flowering of democratic institutions and individual freedoms. The impressive compulsion of self-referencing social media – which the word Facebook captures so aptly – is a symptom of the primacy we give to self-reification. The notion of non-self is a provocative foil for challenging the self-preoccupation dominating our age and exacerbating its social and psychological estrangement. The psychology of non-self offers an alternative view for considering that the self we invest so heavily in promoting and defending is a cognitive-affective chimera, a projective identification obscuring our true nature.

In being gripped by experience, whether we are magnetized, repelled or indifferent to it, we may not be aware we are the one doing the gripping. Thus we become lost in the eddies of our reactions, solidifying the flow of experience as we lose touch with the basic awareness within which all this is happening. Of course, we are also always free to relax our reifying propensities and *not* freeze our stream of consciousness by identifying with this, rejecting that and ignoring the other thing. But just because we are fundamentally free does not mean we are prepared to accept the untethered nature of that freedom. Holding fast to the security arrangements which our self-identity and habitual coping patterns seem to provide, we are left with the dilemma of wanting to be free but not wanting the vulnerability that goes along with true freedom.

Although no independent self may exist, self-centered patterns of reactivity continue to operate both inside and outside our awareness. In order to recognize reactive coping fixations, it is helpful to disentangle the reactive process through which we tangle ourself up. This includes warming-up to the paradox that we are neither the same as nor other than our experience.

Buddhist psychology identifies five psychodynamic constituents which give rise to the self-illusion. Movies are a metaphor commonly invoked to depict how this works. Although a movie is made up of a series of frames with a little gap separating each one, it gives the impression of being a unitary whole. Buddhist psychology unpacks the phenomenology of the self by exposing the gaps between constituents that give rise to this illusion.

While Western psychology generally favors personality theories based on the assumption of a unitary self, there are notable exceptions that lend support to a non-unitary self psychology. David Hume (1978/1739) in particular, proposed a *bundle theory* of the self. In discussing Hume's idea, Evan Fisher explains that, "instead of there being a concrete unified self, there is only a bundle or collection of different perceptions, which succeed each other with an inconceivable rapidity, and are in perpetual flux and movement." (2017, p.58) Hume's understanding turns out to have a remarkable congruence with the Buddhist psychology of non-self.

Non-self psychology

The mind is merely the movement of thoughts and memories;
It has no nature; it is the dynamism of wind energy.
Empty of essence, it is like space.   — *Naropa*

Allowing that no self-entity exists either outside or inside the flow of experience is certainly a radical notion, especially in light of the fact that there certainly seems like there is a *me* reading, questioning and contemplating this idea. To address this conundrum, Buddhist psychology breaks down the process of psychic experiencing, detailing how self-reification occurs. As Fisher notes, even though an independent self cannot be located, the illusion of a unitary self coagulates through a dizzyingly rapid cascade of mental-emotional functioning. Through training in meditative awareness, it is possible to slow the movie-like coagulation process and see how we are, moment-to-moment, fabricating a self-centered "reality." The fictional nature of the self will remain theoretical until we discover the truth of it in our own experience. Through careful self-examination, it is possible to see that what we take to be a solid self is actually an interactive dynamic of psychic bundling, or aggregating, that reifies the energetic flux of experience into static fixations.

As a process of aggregation, five constituents (*skandhas*) dynamically interact, giving rise to that impression of completeness by which a sense of self seems real and enduring; but in actuality is an ephemeral composite of impersonal psychic functions. As the Japanese philosopher, Nishida put it, "It is not that the individual possesses feeling and the will, but rather that feeling and the will create the individual." (Quoted in Pattison, 2000, p.202) Michael Thompson elaborates, "When all is said and done, the choices I make, whether consciously or unconsciously, are not determined by me; rather they determine who I am." (2017, p.188) Emotional reactions captivate *me* to the extent I identify with *them*. Taking ourself to be the reaction – opinion or feeling – we are having, rather than the sensitivity that allows us to have an opinion or feeling, is the way we lose touch with the true nature of human sentience.

The five psychic constituents include: *form* (*rupa*), *feeling* (*vedana*), *emotional perception* (*samjna*), *mental formations* (*samskaras*), and *consciousness* (*vijnana*).

Together, these elements co-condition mental-emotional reactivity that, compulsively repeated to the point of habituation, congeal and propel the psychic formation we identify as *me*. Since these constituents aggregate *en masse*, they behave like a mob, lacking connection and responsibility to their original, uncontrived nature. In aggregating, each constituent loses itself in the other, gets into each other's business, and eggs each other on with a mob-like mentality. Maybe *I* behave impulsively like a mob rioting in the streets in lashing out recklessly. Or maybe I function as if I have it all together, like an apparently civilized, well-managed mob run by a Mafioso or corporate board of gangsters pushing a bottom-line agenda of us against them. Or maybe I shuffle along zombie-like as part of a conforming, anonymous herd that compulsively thinks this way, not that way, feels like this, not that, acts like this, not that. It is debatable which kind of mob causes the most confusion, suffering and regret to a sensitive psyche: the anarchists in the street; organized mobsters skulking in shadows or in the broad daylight of corporate boardrooms; or the everyday herd-mentality congregating on social media and vulnerable to stampede.

This self-aggregation process can be understood as a five step developmental sequence in the direction of increasing self-reification. It can also be appreciated as an interactive process occurring on the fly, all at once. If it is considered as a graduated process of self-fixation, a gradual de-construction and unwinding makes sense in order to free ourself from compulsive reactivity. If it is engaged as happening all at once just now, non-gradual release becomes possible just now. I have found that the gradual, developmental approach is most useful for helping the mind understand how it ties itself up. By the same token, I have found it is only possible to actually free ourself – if only for one sweet moment – if we let go *just now!* Waiting until tomorrow to risk opening ourself is waiting for a day that never arrives.

Self-reification

self is not different from non-self
– Diamond Sutra

Within the developmental approach, *form* (*rupa*) is the first link in a process of experiencing that launches a chain reaction bent in a direction of self-world reification. In the phenomenology of perception, *form* simply refers to the appearance of something which provides the occasion, but not the necessity, of inaugurating an object/subject split. Form is synonymous with the body and the physicality of existence we perceive through the five senses. However, within Buddhist Psychology the body is not split from the mind but bears inherent sentience, as Merleau-Ponty (1962) and a number of phenomenologists also recognize. Sensory perceptions appear with a dazzle and our awareness rushes out, bending to see, hear, taste or otherwise meet them. This outward rush, quite innocently, results in an incipient partitioning and dislocation of awareness. Since what we perceive is filtered according to the contours of our human vision, including psycho-neuro-mammalian filters, that, out there takes shape – form – in here. Again, we are not usually aware of our complicity in the shaping of experience, mistaking an internal *for-mation* for an external perception existing in objective reality. This primary twist is how the process of projection begins, marking the inception of dualistic vision. This rudimentary split happens so quickly we do not register that anything of import has happened at all, even as fascination with "it" leaves us in a kind of bewilderment. For example, walking home late at night on a lonely street, a blur of movement catches my eye from the shadows of a dark alley I am approaching: hoo!

Super fast on the heels of an appearance comes a *feeling* (*vedana*) in regard to that. This second constituent marks the beginning of an emotional reaction. We reflexively feel good, bad or indifferent toward whatever form appears. *Feeling* arises as we find ourself quickly inclined toward, away from or uninterested in whatever is happening. Our feelings may also be mixed, thickening bewilderment. Whatever feeling we have is felt as an emotional jolt. To continue the example, the impression of seeing a dark shadow immediately gives rise to a feeling of apprehension, and my body involuntarily tenses.

A feelingful jolt rapidly morphs into a stronger perception, but not a mere perception arising as wonderment. The third psychic constituent involves a colouring, pre-judiced reaction of *emotional perception* (*samjna*). This is experienced as a mood that comes over us, lending emotional heft to mere feeling, amassing as a more pervasive sense of feeling pleasant, disturbed or vacant.[10] A bad feeling congeals into fear or anger, a good feeling into desire or infatuation and a neutral feeling settles into indifference or boredom.

In terms of physiological psychology, the psychic functions of feeling and emotional perceiving correspond to the limbic system. This perceptual-affective tag team contributes to a rudimentary objectifying of perception, nominating a perceived object as separate from a perceiving subject. Experience gains reifying momentum as emotional associations swiftly well-up under the threshold of consciousness. It is at this point that we may feel triggered and the twin engines of hope and fear start firing, as our limbic system reminds us of similarly resonating past experiences. Old body memories arise, perhaps evoking a strong emotional reaction. In our example, the mere sight of a shadow flitting in a darkened alley throws me into a trembling, cold sweat. Out of what had been a vague feeling of apprehension, I find myself gripped, heart pounding and muscles tightening, veering toward panic. So far, this knee-jerk reaction has developed without my consciously thinking about it. But not for long. Motivated by fear, the discursive mind comes online, racing to figure out what is happening.

The urgency to make sense of a disturbing reaction motivates us to think fast to dispel our increasingly fraught bewilderment. Tacit or vivid memories, whether traumatic or rewarding, anticipations of future scenarios, be they hoped for or feared, the upwelling of self-protective reactions, and associations of all kinds to what is happening speedily come into play. In this fourth constituent, *mental formations* (*samskaras*) arise creating a circular feedback loop between raw emotion and mental images. This mentation may well be subliminal, like idle daydreams in which we are not vividly awake to what we are dreaming or even aware that we are dreaming. We are nevertheless mentally preoccupied, carried away in thoughtforms that are only on the threshold of awareness. Meditative attention may observe such subliminal thinking as undercurrents of thought. Trungpa spoke of this as "subconscious gossip," which aptly captures this kind of mental nattering.

The mind thus charges it projections – hopes and fears – with energy rebounding on the projector, confirming the sense of a self besieged, allured or bored by what is construed to be "really" happening. With calculative thinking mobilized, the sense of duality between me and he, she or it increasingly solidifies in the formation of mental constructs. This marks the beginning of what could further develop into either a vicious or virtuous circle, depending on how we have been habitually coping with things. In the example at hand, my fear of the dark shadow escalates into terror as I think there may be a mugger or rapist lurking in the alley.

---

10 Emotional perception (*samjna*)is similar to Heidegger's understanding of *befindlichkeit*, which Eugene Gendlin translated as felt sensing, a key aspect of his experience-near therapy technique of Focusing.

The reification process continues as mental formations develop into interpretations that become elaborated into scenarios readied to be acted upon. The fifth psychic constituent of *consciousness* (*vijnana*) corresponds to the way Edmund Husserl understood it: "consciousness is always consciousness *of*." (1962/1913, p.222-224) The Sanskrit word *vijnana* is composed of the prefix *vi-*, which means to "sever," or "divide," and *jnana* (*yeshes* in Tibetan), referring to awareness as such, or undivided consciousness. While the notion of consciousness/*vijnana* is quite common in Western philosophical and psychological thought, *jnana* as nondual awareness is less so. The key distinction is that consciousness in both Buddhist and Western thought typically means divided consciousness predicated on a subject-object split; consciousness of, rather than consciousness as such.

Serving as the CEO of the aggregates, consciousness is the executive that makes sense and nonsense out of experience. At this point in the psychic chain reaction, whatever we become conscious of is taken to be distinctly other than the consciousness in which it appears. As the executor of self-identity, it is consciousness that defends, promotes and perpetuates the sense of separate selfhood. As conscious beings, we are captivated by the meaning we impute to experience, cohering a bundling process that reifies a self-world illusion.

Everyday consciousness

The ordinary mind is a good servant but a poor master.
— *John Prendergast*

Everyday consciousness can either be an inescapable enemy or a good friend, depending on whether we lose ourself in compulsive thinking or deploy conceptual thinking in the service of non-conceptual clarity. As *vijnana*, consciousness includes conscious, preconscious and all forms of unconscious cognizance such as appear in the metapsychologies of Freud and Jung. What these psychologies consider to be unconscious are emotional-mental contents that have been either deliberately suppressed or involuntarily repressed; remaining *in potentia* within the (divided) consciousness of a self-referential mindstream.

Extending the hypothetical scenario, let's say that since I have previously been the victim of a violent crime and, traumatized due to that brutality, I have taken the precaution of carrying a firearm for self-defense. Primed and ready to meet an assailant, and finding myself trembling, not just with fear but also with a heightened sense of helplessness echoing from the past, I reach into my bag, firmly grasping the gun. A toxic mix of terror and rage overcome me as I involuntarily flash on the cloudy eyes and foul breath of the rapist I've tried to forget. Raising the pistol in the direction of the emerging shadow, a man turns the corner. I do not remember deciding to pull the trigger. I do remember the shock in my good neighbor's eyes as the gun discharged and he gaped at me, dropping to the sidewalk; a flood of horror bursting over me....

Within divided consciousness, conclusions are reached and actions taken as we react for or against or indifferently to what we think is happening. Consciousness is the function that weaves percepts and concepts together into a story creating a meaningful myth to live by. Stephen Hawking and Leonard Mlodinow speak of this as "model-dependent realism." It is "based on the idea that our brains interpret the input from our sensory organs by making a model of the world. [Which we then] attribute to it...the quality of reality or absolute truth." (2010, p.7) But the interpreted world is neither real nor absolutely true. The meaningful wholes the mind conjures are not whole, but partial to our personal and cultural perspective.

As Carl Jung put it, we exist "only in a world of images, …what appears to us as immediate reality consists of carefully processed images." (Quoted in Fisher, 2017, p.54) Images here should be understood not only in the narrow sense of visual forms, but, once again, in the broad sense of imagination, including the envisioning of personal and social worlds. Recognizing the psychological construction of the human world, Jung is among those psychologists and philosophers in accord with Buddhist knowledge, understanding that we see ideas of reality rather than reality as it is.

In harmony with the psychoanalytic notion of the unconscious as a repository of repressions beginning in childhood, the Buddhist psychology of mind goes further, recognizing a deeper level of (un-)consciousness. This deeper level is the *alayavijnana*, which means *ground consciousness*. It functions like ground in being a fertile field into which are sewn the (karmic) seeds (*vasanas)* of gross repressions which psychotherapy deals with, as well as more subtle psychic imprints, perhaps lingering from past lives. These include positive seeds that are not repressed exactly, but not yet realized either. Existing as latent propensities, both gross and subtle seeds sprout through the threshold of consciousness as *feelings, emotional perception* and *mental formations.* Either when external conditions elicit them or when they ripen on their own and spontaneously come up.

Both stressful and exciting situations can provoke emotional reactions. A provocative occasion might arise in dealing with frustrating technology, a difficult person, an infuriating bureaucracy, or any of the *10,000 things* that mess with us to the point of inciting our anger, lust, fear or helplessness. A triggering of imprints could also occur as something happy, like falling in love, getting married, gaining recognition, having a child, economic windfall or any marvelous occasion that deeply moves us. Either way, evocative situations that break through our everydayness act like moisture and sunlight on karmic seeds, causing them to sprout as we react in possibly unpredictable ways. Unlike the Jungian notion of the Collective Unconscious composed of transpersonal, species-wide governing principles (archetypes), the psychic propensities within the *alayavijnana* are somehow quite personal and unique to our mindstream. If we are able to handle the upwelling in being evoked, it often feels like what comes up needed to come up in order for us to more fully release something we may not even have known we were holding.

A word on karma

> There is no samsara apart from
> your own thoughts and reactivity.
>
> — *Nagarjuna*

Karma, which means "action," or more accurately, *reaction*, simply refers to the law of cause and effect applied to volition: *triggered by that, I react like this. And, having reacted like that, this results.* Fortunately, since there is no fixed self in self-reaction and emotional reactions are transient, even if habitual, the consequences of karmic reactions can be reversed. An aggregating self-in-the-making process also allows for a de-aggregating and unwinding of self-making. This clears the way to recognizing the self's essentially open nature. As Trungpa notes, "Karma is created from failing to see true ego-lessness. It results from the vicious circle of continually searching for security." (1972, p.100) And as Tsoknyi Rinpoche amplifies,

> Mind, or consciousness, is called so many things: soul, spirit, mind, heart. Buddhism defines it as that which knows.... In Buddhism, the term "life" refers to this mind, not to the physical body. There is a continuity, an ongoing sense of knowing, of being awake, that goes on life after life.... It is this stream of life, this stream of knowing, that needs to be liberated. (1998, p.57&58)

It must be admitted that the idea of a mindstream bearing karmic seeds that endure through time, including continuing through death into other lives, seems to contradict the Buddhist notion of a non-enduring self. However, this does not contradict the paradox that even though a separate self cannot be found, cognizance as such, including the functioning of memory, is uninterrupted. Delving deeper into this paradox brings us to a more subtle appreciation of how *I* am able to see that *I* do not exist, being neither this ("I") nor that ("not-I").

Attending more carefully to the functioning of consciousness confirms the psychology of the aggregates. The propensities that give rise to individual differences and unique personalities persist through time only in being bundled together. The continuity of an individual stream of consciousness is accomplished through psychic holding. Karmic seeds are obviously not physical like plant seeds. They persist as psychic propensities due to the pressure we exert, perhaps quite subtly, to keep things under control. The subtlety of this deep holding within the *alayavijnana* is so delicate as to be likened to the remnant scent of perfume in a bottle that has been emptied of its contents. Even though the perfume is gone and not a drop remains, its fragrance persists.

Subtle holdings are the *grounds*, in both senses of the word, we cling to that give shape to conscious awareness. The imprints of karmic residues persist until we release the implicit tendencies through which we are, unawares, holding ourself together. How this persistence (of time) continues after death is certainly a mystery. And if we have our hands full with the problems of this life, the question of rebirth may not matter anyway. But for those who experience an inexplicable evocation of one sort or another, and think the upwelling may be left over from a past life, it may be reassuring to consider that anomalous experiences may not be "crazy" and in need of suppression, but natural arisings to befriend and more fully release.

Disentangling self-entanglement

Awareness is without choice, without demand,
without anxiety; in that state of mind, there is perception.
— *Bruce Lee*

The example of the shadow emerging from the alley illustrates the development of reactivity as a causal chain moving from *form* and *feeling* through *impulsive perception* and *mental formations* to *consciousness* and into action. In this, the conditioned reaction resulted in an expression which manifested in a fight rather than a flight, freeze or please reaction, any of which could have been enacted. As Bugental echoes from a Western perspective in tune with non-self psychology, "The *I-process* is the person be-*ing*, which is expressed through the person act-*ing*, speak-*ing*, and so on." (1978, p.133) The Buddhist psychology of the aggregates describes just this *I-process* explicated to a finer degree of specificity. Since *I* am not fixed anywhere in this active/

reactive process, it is possible – to the extent I am able to pause the reification process – to defuse a potentially compulsive reaction.

For instance, if I could notice my bodily tension as apprehension turning into fear upon seeing a shadow in the alley, I could interrupt the reactive sequence right there by noticing that and taking a calming breath. Pausing the cogitating mind slows the speed of past associations, even as I involuntarily flash on what happened when I was once assaulted. Within this decidedly vulnerable, but less impulsive space, I am less captivated and more able to focus on what is happening in the moment rather than the echo thundering from the past.

Let's say that by virtue of the mindfulness training and therapeutic reflection I have done, I know I am susceptible to misinterpreting these kinds of cues. I know I need to breathe deeper when I get triggered, keeping my senses alert and mind nimble. Being more in touch with the fear and rage threatening to flood my system, it becomes possible, quite literally, to *come to my senses*. Drawing down the energy going to my head on the verge of reactivating an old story, I may feel my body tensing and notice my hand is already groping for the gun in my bag. Whether or not I actually grasp the pistol, I will be more mindful about it as the shadow emerges into the light. Less compelled by an impulsive reaction, I recognize my good neighbor and, tension dissolving, greet him with no small relief.

Compulsive sequence of reactivity

dualistic vision (form) > feeling
> emotional perception > construct formation
> divided consciousness > karmic reaction

Sequence unwinding reactivity

mindful awareness > de-constructing mental formations
> loosening emotional perceptions > feelingful self-awareness
> unformulated openness > unconditioned response

Within mindful presence, the link between obsessive thinking and compulsive reacting naturally dissolves. We can downshift from reactive to non-reactive awareness by mindfully noticing what is happening, reflecting on the thoughts that arise in regard to that, and perhaps diffuse a potentially impulsive reaction. Deepening self-attention, we open to the emotional charge driving our system and are more able to relax compulsive thinking-reacting by attuning to the felt sense of the whole thing. The process of de-constructing self-formations defangs reactive impulses, whether they tend in the direction of expression or repression.

The stuff of dreams

> Know all things to be like this: a mirage, a cloud castle, a dream, an apparition. Without essence, but with qualities that can be seen. — *Samadhiraja Sutra*

The self is nothing but a phantastic process of sensory and imaginal awareness in motion. Thoughts think, feelings feel, sensations sense. The actual nature of the mind is a dynamic motility accruing to no one, innately intelligent and intrinsically free. As Ken McLeod puts it, "Mind is not a thing. Mind is experiencing. Where does experiencing come from? That is the mystery of being." (2001, p.373) Failing to recognize this ineffable openness and innate cognizance, we lose touch with our innermost sense of being and feel, quite rightly, we are missing something essential as we live out our days striving to satisfy an insatiable wanting.

Self-liberation hinges on the ability to tune in to the untethered and unconditional awareness of our basic nature. What is experienced as groundlessness to ego is spaciousness to awareness and boundlessness to an open heart. Whenever there is a pause in the self-grounding conversation we are having with ourself, a gap opens in the chain of reactivity, revealing that who we take ourself to be is a self-world construction project building nothing more solid than cloud castles. Shakespeare put this in the words of Prospero, "we are such stuff as dreams are made on."

Recognizing that what we take to be me, and feel compelled to promote and defend, is nothing but a process of fixation, supports us in not taking ourself so seriously. Allowing that I am not the same as and not someone other than a process of habitual reactivity, supports us in taking our foot off the accelerator of our self-identification project. But also without slamming on the brakes. Of course, slowing down each step of the I-process, say between seeing a form and having a feeling about it, or catching an impulse before it evokes an emotional meaning, is not so easy. Given the speed and engrained habits of the mind, is it any wonder even seasoned meditators and practiced therapy clients find it difficult to notice each link in a psychic chain reaction?

It seems to be more workable to simply acknowledge that psychic constituents are all movements of mind, and instead of trying to focus on a particular aggregate, to attune more spaciously to the mind in motion. This shift is reflected in the evolution of Buddhist psychology (Yogacara) over time. It became clear that, of the five constituents, consciousness is the ground, executor and linchpin holding the whole thing together. All aggregates, psychic holding and emotional reactions occur in a field of consciousness. And they do not necessarily behave in an orderly sequence as outlined, but interact with each other willy-nilly. Marvelously, as the divided propensities of consciousness loosen in slowing down, the other psychic constituents are likewise undermined, and the whole self-reification process buckles. Without fixating, consciousness settles into its natural openness, becoming able to recognize its unbound nature. This non-gradual recognition reveals that self-liberation occurs, when it does occur, all at once just now. When else could it occur?

> Sanity, wholeness, and integration lie in the realization that we are not divided, that man and his experience are one, and that no separate I or mind can be found.   – *Alan Watts*

7

Broken-openness: A portal to authenticity

I tell you one must harbor chaos
if one would give birth to a dancing star.
— *Friedrich Nietzsche*

N THE EFFORT TO SECURE A SELF-GROUND, WE DISCONNECT FROM THE OPEN
ground and its natural resilience. Adopting – in all innocence – a self-de-
fensive posture, correlated tensions congeal in the physical body, energy
blockages in the emotional body and fixations in the mind. Entranced within emotionally-charged thoughtforms, we become captivated by the objects
of our cognition.

The most direct way to see through this confusion is to appeal to naked
experience. It is necessary, as the poet David Whyte puts it, "to slip down
that long branch of your body to the very root and in the earth of your body
hear the damp echo of everything you have not touched." (1992, p.45) This
line captures the emancipatory challenge of the human condition. To be
free, it is necessary to open the repressive barriers defending divided selfhood to the very root. Whether or not we deliberately embark on a path of
self-reckoning, the cosmos can be counted on to present us with the perfect
opportunities for untangling our knots. Of course, what the cosmos presents
may not be the kind of assistance we were looking for.

Befriending vulnerability

Only to the degree that people are unsettled
is there any hope for them.
— *Ralph Waldo Emerson*

From everyday inconveniences like being stuck in traffic or having to
deal with a broken toilet, to big shocks like discovering your lover loves
someone else, you have been laid off from your job, or you or someone dear

to you has been diagnosed with a serious illness, life repeatedly unsettles us in petty ways and brings us to our knees in crushing ways. Whenever we are broken-open by life, we are on a threshold of being shocked out of our illusion of completeness into the crisp lucidity of impermanence. These are the shocks in which Emerson advises we place our hope. The ability to bear the lightness of being is quickened through our willingness to bear its darkness.

For instance, as a perplexed and insecure teenager, I treasured the warm and easy relationship I had with my sister, Stacey, who was the closest person to me during those turbulent years. When I was 19 and living away from home in Atlanta on a co-op job, a business associate of my father's unexpectedly appeared at our door one night, asking me to call home. I was living with other students at the time, and since we couldn't afford a phone line (this was the 1970's), I placed the call in a phone booth on a street corner. Standing under a garish street light, I learned Stacey died that evening in an auto accident. Upon hearing this, the ground I was standing on seemed to give way. In emotional freefall, there was no blow that could have leveled me as totally as that news. I discovered that without Stacey in the world, I was without sure mooring. She was, as Bob Stolorow aptly puts it, my *relational home*. With that home no longer in the world, I was not sure where *I* belonged, and in terms of a self-ground, not sure where I was. At a loss as to how to go forward, I proceeded to wander the rain-soaked streets throughout the night.

While unexpected deaths deliver a devastating blow, all kinds of lesser things happen revealing our existence is not as secure as we would like to believe. We are always and everywhere existentially vulnerable. Even though we routinely succeed in ignoring this obvious truth, unless we are gravely blocked, we do not completely succeed in ignoring our ignoring. Awareness of mortal fragility niggles under the threshold of consciousness. Certainly things don't always go our way. Yet even when things are going well, as they were for me in Atlanta, we may still feel anxious, tacitly aware we are at risk of losing that wellness. This existential sense knows something we would prefer not to know and draws us toward its uncanniness.

Although Stacey's death was personally devastating, it was a totally ordinary event. Even though we know death is normal and inevitable, we lull ourselves into a dull slumber around it. Such everyday ignorance permits this ordinary occurrence to have the effect of a traumatic rupture. Intellectually understanding mortality is still very far from taking it to heart. Once again, in the service of narrative bypassing, conceptual knowledge can feed experience-distant forms of self-deception, in which we think we know something in order to avoid the experience-near pain of emotionally getting it.

Psychology understands developmental trauma and the defense mechanisms that are employed to manage it well enough. We recognize that families may be parented by adults who have not thoroughly metabolized their own internalized fear, aggression and denial, thereby inadvertently impaling their children with their own madness and passing intergenerational trauma down the line. For many, families of origin are complicated and not entirely safe. For those bold enough to look into this mess, it is certainly possible to recognize self and family narratives that have been entrapping, and to crack open the doors of that cage. But looking more deeply into our predicament, we discover it is not just ourselves, our families and our society, but existence itself that lacks the enduring security we long for.

Whatever similarities we share with other sentient beings, Heidegger observed that it is the human being who is "distinguished by the fact that, in its very Being, that Being is an issue for it." (1962/1927, p.32) Wild animals do not suffer the fear of death as we do and give no indication they feel there is anything incomplete or fundamentally wrong with them. But for human beings, accepting wanting and existential vulnerability is the first step in waking up to the way things actually are. In the service of existential sobriety, meditation and experience-near psychotherapy shift from being practices employed to get rid of suffering to means devoted to befriending it.

Pain narratives

The compulsive meanings that fill up our lives are ways of evading a sense of meaninglessness we dread. *– David Loy*

Noting *neurotics suffer from reminiscences,* Freud observed that neurotic symptoms are symbolic expressions of memories we can neither fully remember nor totally forget. The nub of psychological suffering, whether it comes from traumas of ordinary life or from extraordinary traumas of violence, is an unwillingness or inability to relate to experience as it is. As Greg Mogenson puts it, "Symptoms originate in our refusal of them.... No sooner do we say no to life than we are haunted by our unlived life." (1992, p.11 & 12) The Sufi poet, Hafiz, puts it this way, "God is trying to sell you something, but you don't want to buy. That is what your suffering is. Your fantastic haggling, your manic screaming over the price." (1996, p.13) And Eckhart Tolle notes that the refusal to befriend our broken-openness results in our inhabiting a "pain body," which takes shape through the way we engage in the fantastic haggling of compulsive thinking. In order to release the haunting pain narrative that binds us together, it is necessary to pause our self-talk and befriend the pain that drives it.

Even though Atlanta had the highest murder rate in the country the night I wandered its streets, I walked around fearlessly, which was unusual for me. Being a skinny, white guy, wandering aimlessly into poor neighborhoods with clusters of black men hanging around here and there, I naturally drew attention. But I was not accosted in any way. Even at the time I felt that was odd, aware I was in a strange state of mind which apparently evoked some sort of deference.

Reflecting on it later, I suspect the groundlessness of my plight might have radiated a forbidding ethereality. During those hours, I wandered psychically untethered, feeling I had nothing left to lose and nothing conceivable to gain. I imagine that if a "bad dude" did accost me, I would have reflexively looked into his eyes, and stripped-down as I was, peered from the depths of my soul into his. He and I may well have shared a moment, evoked by my naked presence, of genuine contact. If he would have wanted my money, I probably would not have hesitated giving it to him. Not out of fear of being mugged, but because in that moment – which stretched into forever – I felt I had no territory to defend and nothing to hold onto. I was in a state of such broken-openness that I felt no essential difference between myself and others. When Heidegger discusses a moment of authenticity as *being toward death*, he is pointing to just this kind of groundlessness.

The shock of Stacey's death crashed the narrative of me, breaking for a short time the causal chain binding past to future, interrupting my I-process and casting me adrift in The Mystery. Through this, I learned how the curse of heartbreak can be a kind of blessing, but only if it is opened to. We are free to either let experience be as it is or resist what God is trying to sell us. If we can be true to a rude awakening – in the sense that an arrow flies true – this allows for a befriending both of the traumatic pain and the opened-upness the pain has occasioned.

Divine messengers

> I want to know if you are willing to live, day by day, with the consequence of love and the bitter, unwanted passion of your sure defeat.　　　　　　　　　　　　　　　　　　　　*– David Whyte*

A poet, like a therapist, spiritual teacher or your inner truth sense, wants to know if you are willing to authentically show up in your life. If you able to distinguish the clear signal of innate intelligence from the static chatter of the they. If so, are you then prepared to be responsible to it and live that truth forward?

A critical turning point occurred in the life of the Buddha to be, when he left the security arrangements of his family and gated community, deactivated his social media accounts, abandoned his cellphone and computer screens, and proceeded to encounter what he later called the divine messengers of sickness, old age and death. It seems to me these dire messengers are joined by sister emissaries of *anxiety, guilt* and *despair*. Each of these existential envoys is instructive insofar as they alert us to reality as it is. In the service of becoming fully human, each of these unwanted truths is divine if we heed the messages they bring. Since our sense of incompleteness is based on not recognizing our true nature, *wanting*, especially in its more troubling forms, bears a message from the wholeness we have left behind. Like death, aging and illness, anxiety, guilt and despair have an uncanny ability to recall our attention from being dispersed in trivial pursuits. If, that is, we don't get devoured by them.

Existentially-robust therapies recognize that these messengers are portals of authenticity. They bear unique potential for deepening genuine presence by disrupting the complacency of living in everyday distraction. Still, a distinction needs to be made between suffering these states as the existential messengers they are and identifying with them, thereby turning them into *a story of me* and muddling the message.

Fear and anxiety

> Whoever is educated by anxiety is educated by possibility, and only he who is educated by possibility is educated according to his infinitude. Anxiety is the dizziness of freedom.
> – *Soren Kierkegaard*

Anxiety and fear arise when we are up against life's mysteries and find ourself untethered, dizzied by freedom as such. Dizziness in this case is an expression of existential intelligence as long as we are able to tolerate the intensity of groundlessness. Feelings of trepidation remain free and workable until we tighten against them. For instance, an experienced rock climber might not find standing on a precipitous ledge hundreds of feet above the ground to be particularly anxiety provoking. They might even comfortably sleep up there suspended in a hammock. But that same person might find a software glitch, financial loss or unexplained absence on the part of their lover nerve-wracking. A person will be more or less anxious depending on how they take (narrate) the uncertainty of their situation, imagining what might or might not happen rather than being present in the open-endedness of an unfolding situation.

Medard Boss traces the etymology of the word anxiety from *ancho* (Gr) and *angustia* (L), which refer to a constriction, or narrowing. (1990, p.83)

As we know, if we are unable to bear life's unpredictability and essential freedom, anxiety manifests in muscle tensing, holding our breath or otherwise shrinking from being *as it is*. Boss and other Existential psychologists make a critical distinction between *existential anxiety*, when we willingly open to mystery and unknowing, and *neurotic anxiety*, which arises to the degree we brace against uncertainties, mysteries, and doubts (Keats). As the rawness of existential intelligence is stifled, its blockage metastasizes into compulsive thinking. Existential anxiety becomes neurotic when we take it on – in an effort to control it – rather than relate to it as a pulse of nature. We tighten and frighten ourself by elaborating the dizziness of existence into a personal story, as an existential perception turns into a neurotic projection.

Paul Tillich aptly defines neurotic anxiety as that state of mind which "builds a narrow castle of certitude which can be defended and is defended with the utmost tenacity... in order to avoid the threat of non-being, one avoids being." (1952, p.66&76) That is, the neurotic shrinks his world to fit. Attempting to buffer the threats of existence, we try to limit our exposure to it by elaborating a safe self-nest/space suit. Insulating ourself in our thoughts and feelings, we establish what we think is a secure perimeter and patrol our self-world with an anxious eye. Of course, this everyday coping strategy never fully succeeds because we can never fully insulate ourself from existence. Even in the comfort of our self-apart-ment, irritations invariably intrude. Symbolically or in actuality, neighbors play loud music, the smell of exhaust comes through the window, the world's insanity appears in our media feeds, and so forth. As we close our doors and windows, put in earplugs and distance ourself from the immensity of being, we condemn ourself to living in an increasingly claustrophobic world.

Echoing Tillich, Boss confirms the general Existential understanding that "Fundamentally every anxiety fears the destruction of the capacity to be...all anxiety is at bottom the fear of death." (1990, p.77&81) Although this is certainly, for the most part, true, Existential psychology could benefit from looking more deeply into it. While the fear of death comes from the awareness we are going to die one day, that day may be years or decades from now, or it might be later this week or even later this evening. But it is not right now. Since the time of our death is uncertain, we feel anxious. And yet, the nagging suspicion that we do not exist right now is more troubling than dying at some point in the future.

The deeper intelligence of existential anxiety is not only the fear of physical death, but the tacit sense I do not exist as a real entity in the present moment. Orienting our life around a story of me, existential anxiety alerts us to a fundamental flaw in our thinking. Self-narration is not self-existence in the way a map is not the territory. If we look into it, the gnawing sense *something is wrong with me* brings us to a portal – which opens to the mystery, truth and essential freedom of our nature.

It turns out that the neurotic anxiety driving compulsive thinking is an energy source that can fuel our motivation to be free from compulsive thinking. To harness this energy – rather than be harnessed by it – we must befriend our wanting, and to the extent we are capable, open to it by allowing it to open us. To the degree we can play this edge, anxiety naturally releases into unconditional love and trust. Boss puts it this way,

> if one keeps oneself really exposed to the full and undissembled essence of anxiety, it is precisely anxiety that opens… [a] dimension of freedom into which alone the experiences of love and trust can unfold…. anxiety confronts man with the Great Nothingness, a Nothingness, though, which is the opposite of any nihilistic emptiness, which is rather the cradle of all that is released into being. …and opens up the way of love toward the boundless origin of all things." (p.84)

Befriending fear and anxiety loosens psychic holding, opening our fearful heart and giving way to full and deep breathing as compassion for self and other expands.

Both Freud and Existentialists make a distinction between anxiety and fear. Whereas fear is understood as fear of something, existential anxiety conveys the deeper awareness and more elusive disquiet about the no thing of our self-nature. Rather than face the groundlessness of self, compulsive thinking turns anxiety of nothingness into a fear of some thing. By objectivizing a threatening *that*, neurotic anxiety correspondingly strengthens the self-illusion of an endangered *me*. The common childhood (and adulthood) fear of the dark may not be an objective fear, but an anxiety about the unknown, hidden, Great Nothingness as Boss puts it. Having quite a permeable self-membrane, a child transforms the threat of non-being into a monster in the closet. Having succeeded in objectivizing the anxiety, it is more able to be dealt with, as when a parent turns on a light to reveal there is no thing to be afraid of.

The everyday coping strategy of transforming (existential) anxiety into more manageable (neurotic) fear exacts a price. Reifying anxiety into an object results in either a projection onto others or the world, or an introjection into oneself. If projected outwardly, anxiety can give rise to fear, anger, contempt and/or resentment towards *them*. If introjected, as in deciding I am the cause of my anxiety (even if I also blame others for my suffering), I may frighten or become contemptuous of myself. Interpreting the anxious *something is wrong with me* feeling as my own fault further freezes the feeling, forming still more anxiety. And perhaps ashamed and depressed as well, forming a trifecta of self-loathing.

Despair and depression

The danger of despair is that one will cling to it.
– David Loy

As with anxiety, it is crucial to distinguish between existentially intelligent despair that is free-flowing from its neurotically distorted versions that are fixated. Clarifying this distinction has been made more difficult by the muddle of psychiatry in poorly differentiating abnormal states of depression from normal states of sadness, melancholy and despair. As Horowitz & Wakefield (2007 & Bradford, 2013) have discussed, symptoms confirming a clinical diagnosis of depression include sleep disruption, feelings of hopelessness, the inability to feel pleasure, social withdrawal and the sense of having lost meaning in life. These are some of the same things that occur in normal experiences of sorrow, as we suffer life's inevitable losses. The fallout from this professional obfuscation is that anyone suffering and grieving a significant loss is likely to have experiences that qualify as a psychiatric mental disorder.

This muddiness confuses things in two ways. For starters, it blurs the difference between healthy sadness and forms of neurotic depression. Secondly, pathologizing sorrow obscures the possibility that despair, grief and melancholy might have maturational value, are signatures of relational meaning and can open the heart to deeper compassion and wisdom. Since a pathological diagnosis strips despairing states of their emotional intelligence, heartbroken-open states may be rendered valueless, meaningless or even dangerous. Construed as a form of mental illness, despairing persons are influenced to see their emotional state as abnormal; as a mental disorder in need of correction or a chemical imbalance to be adjusted. This view only further reifies the sense *something is wrong with me*. Due to this confusion, psychiatry exacerbates the antagonism between an ideal, non-disturbed self-image, and an awful but authentic lived experience. This muddle makes it more difficult to respect the potential healthiness and transformative value of undergoing a dark night of the soul.

For instance, the shattering I underwent when my sister died changed both my life and benefitted numerous clients who worked with me in therapy thereafter. At the time of Stacey's death, I was just beginning to tune in to the purpose and direction my life could take. Looking back, it is clear that the depth of my grief, including a sense of loneliness that went to the bone, was a critical turning point. Awash in sorrow, I felt the only way I could, in good conscience, live my own life forward was to let the best of Stacey continue to live through the best of me. Bent on drinking and taking drugs at the time, and generally spending my life on self-indulgences, I knew I had to clean up my act. Within a year, I learned how to meditate, stopped using most substances and entered therapy for the first time. In the process of doing so, I found inner work to be a compelling life purpose to guide my own life and to share with others. In this sense, I have never gotten over Stacey's death, and never care to.

As is obvious, experiences of despair, including prolonged sorrow, are at odds with the American gospel of happy, and disruptive to the righteous grind of the Protestant work ethic and spirit of capitalism. Since a period of sorrow may involve a withdrawal from work and business as usual, it threatens both the social illusion that everything is fine – just great! – and the commercial trance that believes constant production, consumption, profit and economic growth are of primary value. So we cannot blame psychiatry alone for wishing to eliminate the pain of despair. Psychiatric diagnoses function as handmaidens to our worldview, operating as instruments of social hygiene serving the status quo. The standard therapeutic goal, "return to previous level of functioning," directs mental health professionals to arrest any dark night of the soul – and evolutionary momentum despair might have – that disrupts everyday functioning.

Religious systems can also serve a social hygienic function. Seeking to be saved or enlightened speaks to *wanting* a despair-free life, in which the nagging sense of incompleteness is filled and *I* am "found." As a true believer conforming to a spiritualized self and worldview, I am temporarily shielded from the feeling there is something wrong with me. A born-again me works (however briefly) by believing in fulfillment rather than suffering the longing for it. Unfortunately, the self-aggression deployed in resisting despair, whether aided and abetted by psychiatry and religion or not, only succeeds in transforming healthy despair into neurotic self-absorption.

Simply put, self-aggression is what neuroticizes normal despair, turning it into depression proper. The term depression perfectly describes what it is and how it functions. *De*-pressing is a willful pushing or putting (ourself) down. Fueled by aversion, depression is another word for a pathetic conversation we are obsessively having with ourself. Even if, and especially if, the self-talk takes place under the threshold of awareness. When I become habituated to a pathetic story of me, a depressing self-narrative comes to define who I am. Appropriated as an identity, depression is taken on as an illness I have or can get. In this passive view, we fail to see that the linchpin of depression is in our repeating a narrative of self-criticism to the point of self-hatred. The heaviness that is felt in and as depression accurately reflects the feeling of our being heavy on ourself. An oppressive state of mind weighs on us, perhaps to the point where it is literally hard to get up and out of bed.

The inevitable defeats and humiliations life provides expose us to the truth of our existential vulnerability. While simple despair involves the conscious suffering of this humbling, neurotic depression is an effort to manage the pain by identifying with a victim position. When we put ourself down by making our story one of *poor me*, the pain of despair morphs into self-pity, blunting its existential message and exacerbating our lostness. As a defensive reaction, depression empowers a resentful self-narrative. The price of wrapping ourself in a blanket of pity is a loss of sensitivity leading to a loss of vitality. Hence depression is clinically classified in the DSM as a mood disorder.

In twisting despair into a depressing self-identity, we become someone we do not like. The pure sadness of having feet of clay and being vulnerable to abuse, rejection, blame and loss hardens into resentment of self (and other) as we refuse to be moisturized by genuine sorrow.

In meeting despair as it is, without making it into a depressing self-story, we do not obstruct it as it moves through our system. When sorrow is neither minimized nor exaggerated, self-centeredness is decentered as we befriend our human fallibility and innate tenderness. Going through a dark night with a modicum of equanimity can be a transformative passage leading to a more vital, less fearful way of living going forward. It is in this sense that *life begins on the far side of despair*, as Jean-Paul Sartre put it. The path of the spiritual warrior, walked with a willingness to be touched by life, evokes the genuine heart of sadness, in Trungpa's words. He (1984/1978) observes that it is human sensitivity, our soft spot, that is always already the precious *bodhicitta* – awakened heart – most prized in Buddhism.

For example, it may be raining and cold outside, or you might be quarantined at home; you are bored, have nothing to do and would like to go for a bike ride. But you can't, so you make a fire, brew a cup of tea and go to the window seat to listen to the rain. Giving yourself such space and a bit of comfort may allow you to open to a strangely delicious melancholy. Life is passing, the sky darkened. You may be alone or with a companion curled up at your feet, or in next room reading; perhaps he is in his sickbed, miserable with the flu, coronavirus or something worse. Steam rises in a wisp from your cup as the fire crackles, the dog twitches, your senses alert, perhaps painfully so, to overflowing. And with surprise, you realize you are awe-struck with an irrational yet poignant gratitude for existence just as it is.

On the other hand, and less graciously, you might want to numb your dreariness and loneliness, even with a companion in the house. Thinking it is too much effort to build a fire or brew some tea, "what's the use?" you slump down in the couch. In search of solace, you eat more than you need to, turn to social media feeds scavenging for "likes," compulsively shop the internet, binge on Netflix or political news or whatever your drug of choice is. You are probably semi-aware of what you're doing, but it's the best move you've got this afternoon, and you don't have a date tonight, and nobody would date you anyway and the rain is a pain to drive in, so why bother going out? If the whole country is also in quarantine, there's nowhere to go anyway. The weather and circumstances, like the gods, like always and most everyone, is against you; probably because you don't deserve any better. Trying to stifle the ache in your heart, you light up a joint or open a bottle of booze, desperate to feel some flicker of well-being. A good part of another day lost in a minor hell. But perhaps all is not really lost, since you can be sure the despair you are just not up to facing today will not abandon you. It will knock on your door again tomorrow or next week, a divine messenger reminding you that although you are just as vulnerable and miserable as you feel, if you let your despair be and move through, without making any more out of it, like everything else in life, it too will pass. And you just might find the stream of *being* in which you swim is more resilient than you think.

Guilt and shame

What is the seal of freedom attained?
No longer to be ashamed of oneself.

— *Nietzsche*

While neurotic anxiety and depression are widely recognized and fretted over, the common woe underlying them – the sense *something is wrong with me* – pervades both as a tacit sense of guilt. Existential psychology is well aware of this, which is why guilt is nominated with depression and anxiety as a third key existential malaise. Like its siblings, it is important to distinguish guilt as a messenger of existential intelligence from its neurotic appropriation as shame. As a portal to authenticity, existential guilt is healthy insofar as it recalls us from being lost in the they, inclining us to be true to our inner sense. It can also be neurotic and unhealthy in the opposite direction, ensnaring us more securely in the shoulds and should nots of a theyself. Existential guilt is authentic as a call of conscience (Heidegger) recalling us to our natural lucidity and as yet unrealized potential, including our caring for others and the world. This is to be distinguished from inauthentic, neurotic guilt, which is not open to the world, but all about *me*.

Boss is once again helpful in noting that guilt comes from the Old English *guildan*, meaning to pay or pay off, and is related to the German, *schuld*, referring to a "debt" we owe the world. (1990, p.80) Authentic guilt is a divine messenger reminding us we are in this world for a purpose we have not yet fulfilled. It is our willingness "to-be-claimed and needed" by the world that we owe to existence. Our conscience supplies us with "a summons and admonition...to be a custodian and guardian of everything that has to appear...in the light of any given human existence." (p. 86) Existential guilt conveys the recognition that we are a servant and shepherd of being, which Heidegger proclaimed to be the essential purpose of humankind. The disquiet we feel as a tug of conscience acts as a summons to tune more deeply into The Question (What am I here for?).

In contrast to authentic guilt which acts as a wake-up call, neurotic, false guilt feeds a self-absorption that cripples the mind and closes the heart. This distinction is well known in general Psychology, insofar as guilt, as a genuine feeling of remorse resulting from something we have done, is distinguished from the shame or self-disgust we feel for who we are in our being. Since the experience of both guilt and shame is one of feeling ashamed, and since it can be difficult to separate guilt over an action from the shame of being the person who did it, I am using these words somewhat interchangeably. I do so in order to highlight the more essential point. The psychological difference between healthy guilt and unhealthy shame is similar to the ontological difference between being true to or divided from our basic nature.

Psychologically, when we respond in a way that is in sync with our truth sense, we feel a lightness, innocence and sense of embodied ease; even if our response is a difficult one to declare. Existential guilt arises when we react out of sync with our inner sense. In this case, we are likely to experience a healthy pang of guilt that recalls us from going too far astray. On the psychological level, authentic guilt is about something we have said or done or left unsaid or undone.

On the ontological level, authentic guilt is a surfacing of the sense *something wrong with me*. This disquiet arises to advise us we have become disconnected from authentic presence. As Loy puts it, "Ontological guilt is the [felt] contradiction between the sense that *I am* and the suspicion *I am not*." (1996, p.55) As an interesting aside, he wonders if the emergence of a separated self-consciousness might be the implicit meaning of the Christian doctrine of original sin. Seen this way, original sin is primal repression; and its sense of wrongness has nothing to do with any moral failing. On this basis, trying to expunge original sin by being repentant, pious, "a good Catholic" and so on, can never succeed. When the ontologically haunting sense that something is wrong with me is taken personally to mean *I am not good enough*, authentic guilt becomes unhealthy and inauthentic, if not toxic. The tacit sense of wrongness becomes reified into the shame of a personal fault. It may be preferable to cling to a shame-based story of me rather than face the way I am a stranger to myself. Just as the groundlessness of existential anxiety is grounded by objectivizing it into specific fears, a lucid opening of true guilt is falsified in being funneled into a personal "searchlight casting for faults in the clouds of delusion" (Robert Hunter).

To the extent we are unready to reliably source ourself from within, we are liable to confuse the call of conscience with admonitions from the they which we have internalized. The suffering of neurotic shame is intensified to the extent we buy into the projections others cast upon us. To the degree we succumb to their projective identification, we live out their confusion, continuing our lostness in the they. Identifying with false guilt, instead of reifying a "poor me," toxic shame reifies a "bad me." Identifying with being a bad person rather than having made a bad choice, shame feeds on itself as self-blame empowers an inverse narcissism. William Blake put it bluntly, *Shame is pride's cloak.*

Although authentic guilt feels miserable and toxic shame worse, there can be a perverse kind of satisfaction in it. For instance, during her recovery from a sex and porn addiction, Erica Garza (2018) describes a particularly intense relapse in her memoir, *Getting Off.* "The adrenaline racing through my body made me feel invincible at the time. And the shame I felt afterward was even better." In raw honesty, Garza identifies both the temporary jolt of invulnerability an addictive compulsion can offer, and even better its chaser: an intense hit of personal shame. Abetted by two millennia of institutionalized Christian shame, beginning with an original sin in which *wanting* and woman are to blame, false shame has taken on a moral legitimacy empowering a negative self-ground for both women and men. The jolt of shame Erica observes seems to be a reassuring jolt of ego.

The thing is, whether we respond skillfully in touch with or react poorly out of touch with our inner sense is less important than how we live that choice forward. If we come to regret an unskillful word or action and dwell on self-blame around it, we further harden our heart. But if we recognize our erring for what it is, honest guilt arises as an inherently moral corrective inspiring us to make amends and track truer to our inner compass. Recognizing our human fallibility, feeling the genuine anguish of it and sincerely resolving not to repeat the erring, the final challenge of healthy guilt (informed by Buddhist psychology) is to let the whole thing go and ourself be as we are, free and fallible.

8

The arc of healing:
From self-understanding to self-liberation

To study Zen is to study the self,
To study the self is to see through the self,
To see through the self is to be liberated by everything that happens.
— *Dogen*

A MAN AND WOMAN SET OUT ON A JOURNEY OF PROMISE AND DANGER IN search of truth, peace and freedom. The man is blind, the woman lame. This partnership is a metaphor of how we walk a path toward wholeness. Sometimes it is framed as two men, other times as a man and a horse. But in every version the pair bears their respective afflictions and cannot make the journey alone. They can only proceed in cooperation. The crippled seer transported by the blind but capable walker. His legs convey as her vision directs their steps.

The Buddhist sense of this partnership suggests it takes both insight and skillful means, including compassion, to fully awaken. Whether working on ourself or with others, we need to have both a clear sense of where we are going (here) and the capability of actually getting there (just now). As necessary as it is, having a sober understanding of the human predicament and intuiting our undivided, true nature is not enough. Insight that knows where it is going but lacks the capacity for getting there gets nowhere. Therapeutic and spiritual skillful means that have the capacity to take us somewhere but do not know where there (naked awareness) is, do not know where they are going. As difficult as it is to accept, understanding that I am my main problem is the easy part. Letting go of the illusion of completeness and clinging to a self-ground is another thing altogether.

True healing and two truths

> True healing nearly always involves the reopening of old
> wounds, the death of illusion, and a courageous confrontation
> with our pain...indicating that our healing process is intensify-
> ing, not stalling; that we are actually more awake and sensitive
> than ever, more deeply connected with the here and now, less
> willing to look away.   – *Jeff Foster*

On a spiritual path, the arc of healing extends from loosening gross
emotional reactions and confused mental fixations to liberating more subtle
tensions separating us from being as such. In a psychological context, Bugental outlined an arc of therapy goals extending along "a span from helping
the client to be more comfortable to a total reconception of the nature of
one's identity." (1978, p.2)

If a person wants only to function better in the world and be more comfortable in samsara, upgrading neurotic suffering to everyday unhappiness
may be enough. With this ordinary motivation, encouraging deeper opening
and risking more radical freedom is beside the point. Like Apollo 13 in its
afflicted flight to the moon, perhaps it is enough, more than enough, for a
person in emotional distress just to get back to the Earth of average everydayness, and continue pursuing the usual worldly concerns. As it was for
the Apollo 13 astronauts who fixed their damaged spaceship with duct tape,
therapy, meditation and religious ritual that function like duct tape might
be sufficient when one just wants to get back to normal. If "going deeper,"
including seeing through the self-illusion, remains only a therapist or spiritual director's agenda, that may well be a display of therapeutic or spiritual
aggression. Why prescribe, or submit, to surgery if a band-aid will do? But
for those who are not content with papering over the pain of wanting, duct
tape will not work. Those divinely stricken, who cannot ignore the evolutionary itch and who are compelled to venture beyond the moon as it were,
in search of a more radical freedom, have to either dive deeper or remain
haunted by their unlived life.

But even for the most dedicated spiritual seeker, diving deeper brings up
the ambivalence that we both want and do not want to be free. True healing
and the prospect of liberation sound like a good idea all the way until we are
actually up against the inner contradictions we have done our best to ignore.
Having to reckon with the shadow (Jung) of our self-image drops us into the
ego-humbling that comes with depth psychological work. And from there
it gets worse.

Without an appreciation that relative (divided) consciousness arises from absolute (undivided) awareness, neither therapy nor meditation will be able to dispel our fundamental self-deception. No matter how long we meditate, do yoga or therapeutically work on ourself, it will never be enough. Freud understood this, implying that psychoanalysis could be interminable. Buddhism also admits as much when it says enlightenment can take three incalculable eons. (Which is a little overkill, since one incalculable eon ought to get the point across!) This is a straightforward admission that on a gradual path, liberation takes forever. Even with life-changing breakthroughs – whether occurring on cushion or couch – we emerge only partially healed, finding ourself still subtly or not so subtly wanting. This is because as long as we are doing therapy, yoga, a specific meditation practice or any self-improvement project, we are not being true to our already perfected nature. Again, the difference between intentionally doing inner work and being nakedly present is the crucial ontological distinction to keep in mind.

Informing this distinction are the two kinds of intelligence which in turn support two levels of truth. Whereas the doing of inner work cultivates truths relative to a doer, a doing and something to be done, the absolute truth of being is beyond, prior to and intrinsic to, whatever we do or do not do. Opening to absolute truth is beyond any self-grounding reference points, including notions of personal progress or regress. The truth of unconditional presence turns us inside out in a freefall of openness. This is not for the faint of heart, as the Buddhist seer, Nagarjuna, makes plain.

> The teaching of Buddhas is based on two truths: an everyday,
>   relative truth and a deeper, absolute truth.
> Those who do not know the distinction between the two cannot
>   know the profound depths of the Buddha's teaching.
> Without accepting everydayness as it is, its deeper truth cannot be
>   pointed out or comprehended, and nirvana cannot be attained.
> [But,] Misunderstanding absolute truth destroys a slow-witted
>   person, like a snake wrongly held or secret knowledge
>   misapplied.
> Thus the enlightened one was cautious in teaching the Truth,
>   knowing those with feeble insight might wrongly conceive it.
>   – *Mulamadhyamakakarika XXIV: 8-12*

In their own ways, depth psychology and Buddhism understand that our desire for freedom must be balanced with our need for security. There must be a *readiness* on the part of a person to face the illusion of the self in opening to groundlessness. Otherwise, a seeker is liable to make a serious error, mistaking a relative, constructed truth for the unconstructed real deal.

Even though we may be able to see through some of the hypocrisy of consensus reality and conventional morality, that does not mean we have seen through the seer of this insight. Without an ability to rest in untethered openness, self-knowledge still binds the knower to the context – ground(s) – of the known. As useful and illuminating as relative knowledge is, in remaining bound by the known, the creative intelligence and compassionate viscera of unconditional presence cannot fully flower.

Two glitches

There are two common glitches in the process of opening up related to the two truths. One occurs when a clear glimpse into the selfless nature of mind occurs but is re-obscured, as we quickly grasp again after objects, meanings and projects to reground a self-sense. This is an indication that while we may be able to briefly open ourself, we lack the capacity to more fully dissolve self-grounding compulsions into their empty-open nature. The other glitch, which Nagarjuna highlights, is more serious. In seeing through the self-illusion, but being unable to rest in the openness of the seeing, we imagine we have achieved a liberation that has already slipped away. Thinking "I have had an enlightenment" is a concept that has already lost touch with the recognition that I was the illusion seen through. Buddhist psychology considers this self-deception – taking emptiness/non-self as real – to be more dangerous than getting re-entranced in a theyself. It is more dangerous because thinking "I know The Answer" further – more proudly – distances us from The Mystery.

Even so, either glitch – if recognized – can be a divine messenger, revealing the need to strengthen our capacity for befriending untethered openness. In order to better bear/bare authentic presence, psychotherapy and contemplative practice have developed an array of skillful means for playing the edge between vulnerability and self-protection. In Buddhist practice, true healing allows for and proceeds to integrate both truths by respecting that the way of doing so involves two oscillating phases.

Two phases

Strengthening the capacity for bearing the lightness of being proceeds in the play – in the sense that a hinge has play – between being overwhelmed by openness and stifled by our security arrangements. The understanding emerging from trauma work speaks of titrating post-traumatic stress reactions by remaining within a manageable "window of tolerance." This refers to an optimal range of vulnerability, in which we are able to open to what comes up but not so much as to be flooded by it. Contemplative traditions have not developed this therapeutic specificity, but have general guidelines for modulating self-attention in a way that neither pushes too hard nor avoids too much. The classic Buddhist meditation instruction advises opening to the flow of experience in the manner of tuning a stringed instrument. If agitation or fear arises, the instruction is to loosen the tautness of attention. On the other hand, if drowsiness or dullness arise, it is best to tighten the strings of attention by concentrating more sharply. Ideal meditative awareness is when our attention is supple and alert, neither too tight nor too loose.

Respecting this need to modulate openness, Vajrayana Buddhism conceives of the spiritual path as having two phases. The first involves a *phase of preparation*, or *development*. This phase aims to strengthen our capacity for befriending confusion and tolerating ambiguity. On this basis, a *phase of completion* involves opening to unknowing, releasing fixations and abiding in untethered openness. The (ontological) difference between these phases corresponds to the two (Mahayana) truths. This is the same distinction informing gradual versus non-gradual spiritual paths.

It should be noted that the Buddhist notions of two truths and two phases, like Rumi and Heidegger's two kinds of intelligence, are all developmental constructs. As such, they are expressions of only one kind of intelligence, truth and phase. Each of these twofold distinctions is itself a display of relative truth, an artifact of conceptual rather than meditative thinking. Paradoxically, these distinctions are made in order to dissolve themselves. A conceptual way of thinking about non-conceptuality is useful, because when we seek true healing we always do so from within a divided, concept-bound consciousness that needs healing. We begin from calculative, everyday thinking that mistakes the relative truth of our self-world as absolute. So, it is practical to respect both the relative truth governing everyday confusion as well as allowing for an absolute truth that expresses a freedom unbound by relative conditions.

The two truths and two phases of the path proceed like an intertwining strand of DNA. One does not exist without the other, like an individual being does not exist apart from *being*, or like images in a mirror do not exist apart from the immutable nature of the mirror. The healing irony is that because of going astray in (mis-)taking ourself to be a divided self, is it possible to see through the clouds of our mistaking and open to our skylike nature.

The most complete healing does not occur by trying to heal ourself or get enlightened, but by opening to ourself as we are: unhealed, imperfect and longing for something more. Only then, by not resisting our sense of lack, will we be able to see ourself as we are, infinite. The groundlessness of self-grounding reveals the ground of being to be in endless, inconceivable flux. As the coda to the Christian prayer puts it, "world without end,

Amen." And as buddha-vision more radically declares, also without beginning. Unborn and unceasing, existence is ecstatic spontaneity through and through. The deepest, truest healing comes from recognizing and resting in this mystery. But practically speaking, we must still discover what our tolerance for openness actually is, and it may be useful to know where we are along the arc of healing.

The arc of healing

Men are disturbed, not by things, but by the principles and notions which they form concerning things. Therefore, when we are hindered or disturbed or grieved, let us never attribute it to others, but to ourselves; that is, to our own principles and notions.   — *Epictetus*

Intertwining Buddhist practice with Existential therapy, Elise Eschen (2020) shares a poignant reckoning in her process of healing.

After my opening at the monastery, I re-stumbled upon the dreaded question, 'who am I'. Instead of becoming open and curious to the question and my process, I used the information I gained from [meditation] practice to shore myself up. I could see how I created and reinforced patterns with depression, and with this insight I concluded, "you shouldn't take yourself or your experience seriously." (Ajahn Chah) Closing myself back-up again, I used my insight to generate knowledge about myself and began self-reifying that 'I did not exist'. For me, this meant that I could continue to deny the confusing events in my childhood and the overwhelming thoughts and feelings I found within.

This was a huge mistake. I did not know that I was actually in a place of resistance and using the teachings to reaffirm the patterns of disassociation, self-hatred and denial that had been with me since I could remember. I used the teachings to deny the things that would arise in my mind and body. I used the teachings to close myself up, telling myself that I should not listen to or take my thoughts or feelings seriously. I could not see that I fell back into old patterns of self-rejection. Without knowing it, I stopped practicing and began to "spiritually bypass". I jumped to the conclusion that I did not exist, nothing I do matters.

Engaging in earnest meditation and picking up nondual teachings is a little like picking up a rattlesnake. If you are too wary, you never do it. If you are too cavalier, you may get bitten. When that happens, what matters is how you tend the wound and draw out the poison, which necessarily begins, as it did with Elise, with self-honesty. As she discovered, opening herself afforded a further opportunity for closing herself. The remedy? world without end: keep opening.

The following sketches portray how a process of opening proceeds from being closed in like so:

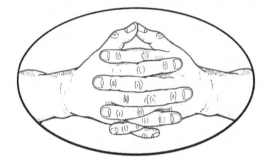

to cracking the self-shell:

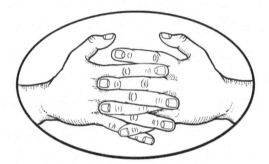

As Bugental portrayed it, this partial opening reflects how a gradual therapeutic loosening of defenses occurs through befriending coping patterns. A little more light gets in, affording a little more freedom and ease.

The thing is, a modest degree of opening allowing for even a little more freedom may be experienced as life-changing and celebrated as a fine therapeutic outcome. But it can also serve as preparation for deeper opening. As Namkhai Norbu Rinpoche suggests, "for some people therapy can be seen as a kind of preliminary purification practice for getting on the path of Dharma." (1994, p.21&22) I would add, not only can it be useful for getting on a spiritual path, therapy may also be helpful in getting better traction when one is firmly on a path. As it was for Elise, who further explains,

Nowadays, my meditation and practice are much different from when I began as a teenager. This is because, through therapy, I have developed a more authentic-accepting way of being with myself, and the things that I find within. I am not as blocked, and my energy has space to move freely. I absolutely had to mend the split within myself before I could practice with ease. Before, meditation was more of a grueling task of concentration. Now it's a game of rest and kindness. Before, I was trying to get enlightened, trying to be present, trying to be anything other than who I am. Now, I'm not trying to do anything at all. Or, if I notice that I am trying to do, or be something, I can put it down. And if I'm really stuck and I can't seem to separate from my energy, it's ok, I can accept that and just be kind. These things sound so simple, but it took me to the brink of suicide before I could finally choose a more authentic way of being.

Within a more expansive vision, the loosening of life-changing therapy and meditation is not an endpoint, but a step toward a more radical freedom like this:

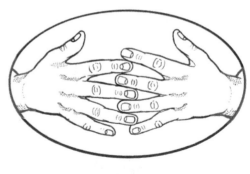

then this:

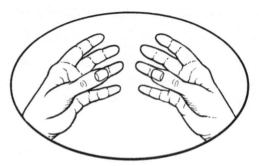

and beyond into empty-openness:

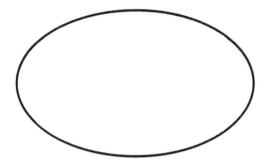

and then to this, an undefended being-in and unhesitating caring-for the world as it is:

This arc of healing illustrates a progressive, step by step process. Defenses are gradually released as we open more nakedly to things as they are. Tensions progressively dissolve as our sense of self becomes increasingly permeable, eventually vanishing into the radiance of enlightened intent.

In contrast to the gradual unfolding of a developmental process/phase, is the lightning flash awakening of the completion phase. Within the now of absolute truth, there are neither two truths nor two phases, no onto-logical difference, nothing to purify or develop and nothing to progress toward. Since *being* has no beginning or end, and no stages to traverse in-between, the completion phase is not a phase, but the whole and goal of self-liberation. Which is why it is said on non-gradual paths, the path is the goal and the goal is the path.

While preparatory phases of self-examination and insight meditation are concerned with self-understanding, acceptance and developing the capacity of self-awareness, a moment of clear, nondual seeing reveals we are already in sync with the wholeness that always already is. In a moment of authentic presence, there is nothing outside of *now* to change, improve or prolong. Both the preparatory and completion phases are devoted to awakening, but the phase that works best in any particular moment depends entirely on a person's capacity for daring naked openness.

On capacity: Being willing and able

> We're not healing illnesses, we're freeing capacities that have
> been constricted. — *James F. T. Bugental*

While non-gradual paths are considered faster and more direct than gradual approaches, whether they work that way depends on our capacity for tolerating untethered presence. To the degree this capacity is lacking, fear, hope or pride intervene, and the fast track is not so fast. Conversely, someone diligently working on a gradual path may ripen their capacity for resting in naked awareness quickly enough if they recognize openness in itself as the goal. The parable of the tortoise and the hare portrays how over-confidence in a person of higher capacity can delay them, while humble perseverance in a person of lower capacity steadily propels them.

When asked what sort of person is most able to attain enlightenment, the Buddha said the best practitioner need not be particularly pious (a good Buddhist), neither is it someone who is especially smart or well educated, and of course a person's race, sex, socio-economic status and personality disposition matter not at all. He said the most able practitioner is the one who keeps going, who makes awakening the most important thing in their life. This speaks to motivation: how deeply do we want to be free? And aptitude: even with motivation, how able are we to open to the vulnerability that goes with that? Like the metaphorical couple mentioned earlier, clear vision and capable legs together determine our capacity for walking a path of self-honesty and liberation.

It is not uncommon for a course of therapy to falter when a therapist has more motivation for a client to change than does the client. The same is true in spiritual relationships. A rule of thumb I adopted as both therapist and teacher, is that if I find myself working harder than my client or student, it is likely that my therapeutic or spiritual ambition is blinding me to the other person's actual capacity. Likewise, when there is deeper work to be done and we avoid delving into it, therapy may slip into nothing more robust than supportive counseling and meditation may plateau into nothing deeper than stress management.

Rather than being an empathic failure, a comfortable therapy can founder as an empathic success. The same thing is true in spiritual relationships. An *empatheosis* occurs when a therapist or teacher is so sympathetic to a client or student they lose themself in the other. While a collapse of personal boundaries may be a proto– sort of nondual presence, and quite delicious (as every lover knows), if we are not capable of resting in untethered openness, the I-process will reassert itself (glitch #1) by slipping into a We-process that sub-merges individuality, stifling true freedom. Merging with an other can temporarily anesthetize the pain of divided selfhood, numbing the inner sense of both partners. In the place of opening more fully to the ache of wanting, a merged sense of *us* tempers existential messages – even if it also facilitates a basking in secure attachment – on a We-ground.[11]

Sometimes this occurs when a course of therapy has run its course and it comes time to leave. It may be easier for both client and therapist to remain in a comfortable relationship than suffer the pain of separation, and learn again what impermanence has to teach.

Similarly, it is not uncommon for meditators who have an established mindfulness practice, to tuck into a meditation routine that manages stress on a day-to-day or as-needed basis, but does not go beyond a stress management function. Over time, meditation practiced in this way is likely to stall in a calm, benumbed state or become boring. When meditation plateaus into a passive routine, contemplative capacity stops growing. If meditation becomes boring, we may think, "Why bother? I'm getting nothing out of this." And then, being still driven by *wanting*, we will seek other, more exciting diversions. Which is too bad, because boredom, as a herald of inattention, is a potent divine messenger. When tuned into, boredom's heaviness is often a resistance against a deeper uneasiness, a "beautiful monster" as Tsoknyi Rinpoche likes to say. A meditator unwilling to befriend boredom and open to what lies beneath, may quit meditating, but will not escape the evolutionary tug that will draw them back to boredom's groundlessness.

Trungpa is refreshingly sober about the dilemma we are up against in seeking true healing.

> We view our desire to get rid of disease as a desire to live. But instead it is often just the opposite: it is an attempt to avoid life. Although we seemingly want to be alive, in fact we simply want to avoid intensity. (1991, p.181)

In order to open more fully to the intensity of existence, it can be useful to have a range of skillful means to apply to our particular situation well-suited to our capacity. While the specific tangles we have to loosen are unique for each of us, the general arc of opening roughly accords to a continuum of deepening self-awareness.

---

11 David Loy playfully speaks of this as a *wego*.

Continuum of Self Awareness

	Objectification — Divided Consciousness (Calculative Thinking)		Subjective Immersion — Undivided Consciousness (Meditative Awareness)		
Unreflective: emotionally reactive, opinionated, mentally fixated	Conceptual reflection: Objectifying experience by naming and describing	Deepening conceptual reflection: Tending toward objectification	Non-conceptual (phenomenological) reflection: Tending toward the subjective	Felt sensing, mindfulness: Subjective inquiry	Nondual presence: Being/subjectivity as such
Self-identified with the story of me	Discerning the story of me = objective content focus	Analyzing the story of me = inward content focus	Opening the story of me through free association/ choiceless awareness = inward process focus	Loosening identification with the story of me through somatic-felt sensing = deepening inner process focus	Disidentification with with the story of me = panoramic awareness (subject-object split dissolves)

Continuum of self-awareness

A continuum of awareness extends from objectifying tendencies of divided consciousness to subjective immersion in being as such. From being unreflective and lost in a theyself, conceptual self-reflection turns awareness around, withdrawing projections and deepening into subjectively-keyed, non-conceptual felt sensing. Indwelling awareness continues to deepen, opening to the liberating mystery of nondual presence.[12]

Waking up from being entranced in a theyself through self-reflection is the first step toward psychological liberation. Conceptual reflection involves thinking about how we are reacting, allowing us to see things more objectively. This includes naming and describing what is happening. It is the beginning of rationally understanding the ground(s) we are already standing on. As understanding of how we are perpetuating our predicament continues to deepen, rudimentary deconstruction of the I-process takes place. A composite example from my therapy practice illustrates how this unfolds.

Bailey began therapy wound up and visibly agitated, having little capacity for self-reflection. He presented his problem as "my wife is impossible, I've just gotta get out this marriage." This description of his predicament is framed objectively. It is strictly content-based and conceptual, concerned with things that have happened in the past and what he wants to do about it in the future. Naming an objective what/presenting problem provides a starting point that allows us to further unpack what is going on by more thoroughly describing it. Through calming down compulsive thinking, conceptual reflection allows Bailey to more clearly identify what "my wife is impossible" means.

Conceptual inquiry might involve making a list of pros and cons to better think something through, but remains on an objective, experience-distant level. This can be quite helpful, for instance, in analyzing what kind of car to buy or investment to make. But it is less robust in untangling subjective and relational issues which elicit mixed emotions. Being more akin to convening a business meeting than a social date, concept-driven reflection is not capable of untangling complexities of feeling, which I discovered at a life-changing moment.

In my late '20's, my wife phoned from across the country to tell me she was pregnant. That news arrived, as it often does, as a full stop Holy Cow! Especially since it was unplanned and untimely. Having just begun a PhD program, I had my hands full while working at a low-paying community mental health job. Having one child already who was well into her teen years, my wife was looking forward to having fewer parenting demands. Money was tight, we were both more interested in doing our own things

---

12 This continuum is informed by the work of John Welwood (2000) and Jim Bugental (1987).

than taking on another 20 years of responsibility for someone else. Underlying all of that, our relationship was not going well. So we decided, each on our respective coasts, to take a few days to think about it.

I dutifully made a list of pros and cons about either terminating or proceeding with the pregnancy. With a line running down the middle of a page, the cons column was quite long. There were many good reasons not to go forward with this. On the pros side, there was only one reason, and it wasn't even a reason. Looking away from the lopsided list, I put my pen down, looked out the window and tuned in to my inner sense. I found my decision had already been made. I knew without a doubt what I wanted/had to do. As I write this, my son, who was born some months later, is considering the same question. As it turned out, that was one of the easiest and best of the big decisions I ever made, even though it made no logical sense.

Before I had fancy words for it, that list-making exercise confirmed for me the critical difference between calculative thinking and felt sensing. This is an example of that ontological difference in which *the heart has reasons of which the mind knows not*. The thing is, although I did not follow the logic of my list, I still needed to make that list. It was only through making and sitting with its cold logic that I was able to realize it was incomplete in an essential way.

Along the continuum of awareness – and reversing the aggregating I-process – naming and describing what we are experiencing clears the space to flesh out richer emotional textures through making meaningful associations. With increasing self-awareness of the connections between past and present, how and why we are living our lives the way we are makes more sense. We become less of a stranger to ourself. Through a process of *tuning in*, reactive coping patterns are better understood, and we can more ably see our craziness is not so crazy. We begin to see that it is not *me* that is the problem, but the way I've been conditioned. We may also see that our habitual defensiveness has been our best, if imperfect, attempt at self-preservation.

Back to Bailey: upon describing the conflict with his wife more thoroughly, he was able to disclose that "'by 'impossible' I mean Gwen argues with just about everything I say. I can't catch a break. She's like my stepmother who gave me shit for everything." To which I reflected, "man, you're up against the same thing." For a person able to sense into feelings, associating to related issues further deepens self-awareness, perhaps surfacing old, undigested pain. This surfacing is no longer strictly conceptual but breathes more fully through forgotten memories, including disappointments, aspirations and trauma. Easing into a more feelingful space, Bailey eventually realized, "Its not that I want a divorce, I still love Gwen and I sure don't want to mess up our kids. But man oh day! Its just so awful."

Knowing that his usual coping style is to withdraw, and that he felt safe with me, I leaned on him a little at this point. Saying, "Well, how would you feel about sharing some of these feelings with Gwen? I wonder if she knows how much you're hurting?" At this, a pallor came over him. Noticing the change, I ventured, "Ah, that hit a nerve." To which he squirmed a bit, and obviously more in touch with what was going on for him around this, admitted, "yeah, its like the air went out of me.... that kinda shakes me up." "You mean thinking about talking to Gwen rattles you?" "Yeah. It's like I'm facing Denise [stepmother]. My palms are sweaty just thinking about it." Regardless of how the relationship between Bailey and Gwen would evolve from this point on, he was now capable of tuning in and being more fluent in expressing his emotional intelligence. And he would soon face the more humbling truth that he defensively avoids conflict not only with Gwen, but with women in general, and often men as well.

Deepening subjective presence involves a progressive loosening of defenses. So, from this point on the continuum, the focus of self-awareness shifts from making sense of things to tapping into the emotional soup underlying that sense and driving the story of me. Opening-up transforms into a process of un-making. From here on, self-reckoning becomes progressively less invested in untangling a theyself in a quest to find and make personal meaning. At this point, the search for psychological authenticity may collapse; and a person will either leave therapy and stop meditating or continue down their inner rabbit hole leading to a kind of existential vertigo. Self-reflection may morph into the question, Who is reflecting?

Deepening meditative attunement shifts attention from the whats of experience, including objects of mindfulness, to the experiencer of those things. This is the pivotal shift that allows for seeing through projections by noticing how experiences – both outer and inner – and the experiencer are not separate things, but a dynamic of inter-being. Upon recognizing there is no independent, totally objective outer experience, it becomes obvious there is no independent self-entity. This is the game-changing epiphany that reveals everything we take so seriously – including life projects of noble purpose – are not as solid as they appear. So we may as well lighten-up.

Back to me again. As the relationship with my wife continued to worsen in the years following our son's birth, we got into more frequent quarrels. In one particularly dreadful exchange we were mercilessly at each other, criticizing and blaming, defensive and offensive, louder and colder and harsher until my body was literally trembling with pain and fury. And just then, a miracle!

Out of the blue, I saw the ludicrous folly of the whole thing; and with the fight evaporating out of me, broke out laughing. Spontaneous presence broke my fear-enraged trance, catapulting me into non-defensive light-heartedness. I assume it was by virtue of both the high energy of the exchange and the Dzogchen I was then practicing, that my system was somehow primed to instantaneously let go. In any case, I had some delightful moments of freedom seeing through myself. Stunned at this outburst, my wife was befuddled, assuming I was laughing at her rather than the absurdity of our argument. Unfortunately, I was unable to convince her otherwise or myself abide long in that moment of happy lucidity. Still, the experience confirmed that the Dzogchen teaching on nonduality is correct. Spontaneous self-liberation is possible, especially if our system is clued-in and ready for it.

When we see that our personal experiencing is not bound to a self-entity, but arises within and passes through a field of self-existing awareness, the separation between subject and object dissolves as we move beyond divided consciousness. The instantaneous recognition of unconditioned presence is in itself the self-liberating practice of letting be: resting in the natural ease, delight and simple freedom of being.

Exercise 2

To what do you devote your life?

Solo inquiry: Ready yourself by sitting in a comfortable position that allows your spine to come into alignment and your breathing to be easy and deep. Slowly take 2 or 3 deep breaths, allowing your energy to flow freely and momentarily clearing your mind. From a place of inner quiet, ask, *To what do I devote my life?*

Note whatever arises. If you wish, jot it down. Then ask the question freshly again; and again... There may be a number of things to which you are currently devoting your life. They may have to do with survival and other worldly concerns and significant relationships. Some you may not be particularly proud of, while others will resonate with a sense of rightness. Whatever arises, let it come and continue to pose the question.

Note the feelings that arise with each item (jotting them down if you like), gauging the extent you feel you are devoting your life to pursuits and relationships that resonate with your best inner sense. Continue until nothing more comes. Then, take a few moments to review what you discovered, sensing how truly you are on course, and if you need to make any course corrections.

Dyad inquiry: Same as above, except done with a partner who simply asks the question, *To what do you devote your life?* without adding any comments, interpretations or evaluations, negative or positive. Continue to repeat the question until the inquirer is empty. Then switch roles. After both partners have inquired, debrief between yourselves and/or with the larger group if there is one.

Part Two

Inside Out

The contemplative yoga of self-liberation

Who looks outside dreams. Who looks inside awakens.
— C.G. Jung

9

Enlightened intent:
The evolutionary thrust towards
well-being

Buddhism explains human beings' higher qualities of intuition, intellect and intelligence; we maintain that human
growth is very different from that of vegetables. Each of us has
a long history; we've been developing a long time, especially
our consciousness.   – *Lama Yeshe*

ONCE AGAIN, DISCONTENT IS NOT ONLY A PROBLEM FOR THE SELF, IT IS A
problem of the self. The way out of troubled states is the way in. In the
search for authenticity, being present to what is rather than remaining
captivated by our stories about it aligns us with the sanity of nowness. And
what is happening just now is nothing less than our participation in the
evolutionary thrust of existence itself. Coming into accord with the flow
of experience pulls together existential estrangements that otherwise splay;
and in splaying, give rise to anxiety, despair and guilt. Relaxing self-reifying
impulses and "leaving behind the empty shell of an isolated self" opens us
to the enlightened intent of the cosmos, which unfolds as a "thrust towards
(well-)Being." (Guenther, 1976, p.52) This spiritual inclination is not other
than the psychological impulse toward radical authenticity, which Bugental
describes as the "degree to which we are at one with the whole of being."
(1981, p.33)

If you think about it, the purpose of all our endeavors – each and every
one – is to arrive in a space of well-being where our striving for fulfillment is
fulfilled. Guenther puts it quite simply, noting that the thrust toward "pleasure is basic to health, whether we understand health in terms of the body
or the mind. Just as illness is the loss of health so any decline in pleasure
represents a lowered state of well-being.... who[ever] is in the grip of his
emotions is in a rather poor state of health, 'out of sorts'." (1976, p.126)

The human predicament is such that we continually miscalculate how
to access true well-being. Getting caught up in seeking pleasure there and
then while struggling against pain here and now, we recurrently find ourself

out of sorts. Thinking that basic well-being can be found in a person, thing, accomplishment or exciting experience to come, we suffer being "out of it." Even when we succeed in getting what we want and enjoy some fulfillment, the vitality of that feeling inevitably passes, and we find ourself again lacking as we strive for something or someone else to fulfill our wanting. Preoccupied with projects of doing, we lose touch with the intrinsic wellness of being over and over again.

On the other hand, by relaxing striving and letting ourself be as we are, we settle more deeply into ourself, and can more readily attune to the vivacity of existence as it unfolds. As we relax seeking something other than what is already happening and stop managing the flow of experience, we allow ourself to be more fully a part of The Mystery. In sync with what is, innate well-being and clarity are likely to arise, rendering our hopes, fears and habitual coping strategies superfluous. Within undivided attention, fulfilling presence organically deepens. We naturally tune in to the tightness in our chest, the zing! in our loins, the knot in our stomach, the breath as it breathes us, the dance of light among shadows, the touch of a breeze on our skin.... Coming back to *this*, we realize we totally belong here, and more deeply feel the transitory textures of experience as well as the immutable awareness in which experiencing takes place.

In difficult situations and disturbing states of mind, tuning-in rather than (re)acting-out enables us to befriend rather than oppose our experience. As Bugental proposed, "authenticity is the letting be of all things human and then finding more encompassing ways of being with all such things." Even in wretched moments, if we can open and rest in the unpartitioned nature of mind, it becomes apparent that whatever is happening has a rightness to it. Whatever is happening is perfect simply because it is what is happening. The isness of experience is always already the ecstatic intent of enlightenment.

> From awareness, uncreated and spontaneously present, arises enlightened intent, a natural state of rest that is effortless and spacious.
> – *Longchenpa*

In discovering this basic sanity, we discover our intrinsic innocence. Without forethought, but responding spontaneously to what is happening by doing what needs to be done and not doing what does not need to be done, we accord to evolutionary intent. Taoists refer to this (ontological attunement) as *tao*, the Way of innate intelligence. Upon emancipating ourself from the dictates of the they and identification as a theyself, we become more able to sync with an intentionality that does not belong to us, but to which we belong. Unlike the inaction of passive withdrawal, and beyond defensive (re) actions, authentic presence yields to enlightened intent through non-action. It seems there is an evolutionary process going on, in which sentient beings are not only biologically adapting to their environments as Darwin and Lamarck discussed, but are also psychically evolving to be in closer accord with the tao. In this view, the tensions we hold in our body and confusions of the mind intrinsically *want* to relax.

Divided consciousness and the intelligence of wanting presents us with a fertile ambivalence totally worthy of respect. We long for security, predictability and satisfaction as well as for the unpredictable *zing!* of ecstatic presence that comes with the insecurity of untethered freedom. We are free to attune to the impulse of authenticity and yield to the vulnerability of greater openness, or not. Although it can be denied, we cannot escape the cosmos' evolutionary itch: the existential disquiet propelling us to heal our divided mind and open to the unfathomable, ever-creative fount of well-*being*.

Upon accepting inner ambivalences, it becomes possible to more deftly negotiate the process of opening-up, balancing self-honesty with self-compassion. It is not enough to merely believe openness and freedom are a good idea; it is necessary to discover if undefended presence can be trusted; if it is feasible to relax defensive postures and suspend self-world narratives that give us a measure of security. No matter how much we read and listen to wise words of liberation, there is only one way to find out.

10

Mandala of self-liberation

Afflictions are great wisdom and, like a fire that benefits a forest, are a yogi's boon.

– Naropa

BASED IN RELATIVE TRUTH, THE ARC OF HEALING PROCEEDS PROGRESSIVELY as the continuum of self-awareness depicts. Cleaning up fixations and softening compulsions occur gradually by withdrawing projections one by one. At the same time, informed by absolute truth, it is possible to see through fixations and reactivity as they arise, allowing liberation to occur immediately on the fly, as it did for me during my marital spat.

The following five chapters unpack an integrative approach to unwinding fixations that has proven indispensable for me and many of those I have worked with. This proceeds according to a fivefold process of *calming down, tuning in, deepening, seeing through* and *letting be*. Although presented as a progressive sequence, don't be fooled. This gradual orderliness is a feint to support a mind not yet ready to open fully to its groundless, evanescent nature. Like a handrail, it is a support for an insecure mind that wants, and perhaps needs, something to hold onto while it bucks up the courage to face the Truth that disperses the need for all such supports, teachings, teachers and tethers. In deference to openness as such, which gulps down every relative truth, it is best to consider these five folds as not necessarily linear, but as an inter-related mandala of liberation. In which any one of these skillful means can elicit any other as evoked by enlightened intent.

Accepting the all too human truth that we want the joy of freedom but not the fear that goes with it, the first three folds involve openings that are pertinent to both therapy and meditation. These involve reckoning in increasing depth with conditioned mindstates. The latter two folds integrate psychological work within a recognition of the unconditioned nature of mindstates. Sequentially, *calming down* is a foundation for being able to *tune in* to felt experience, which allows for *deepening* felt immersion. Within deepened presence, *seeing through* the self-illusion becomes more viable; which in turn allows for *letting* unconditioned presence *be*, such that it more thoroughly saturates our system.

11

Calming down

Research has shown again and again that compassion leads to a successful and fulfilling life. Why, then, do we not focus more on cultivating it into adulthood? When we're angry, our judgment is one-sided, as we aren't able to take all aspects of the situation into account. With a calm mind, we can reach a fuller view of whatever circumstances we face.

— Tenzin Gyatso, 14th Dalai Lama

One large caveat

Man is very well defended against himself, ...he is usually able to perceive of himself only his outer walls. The actual fortress is inaccessible, even invisible to him, unless his friends and enemies play the traitor and conduct him in by a secret path.

— Nietzsche

GIVEN THE SNEAKINESS OF EGO, IT IS AN INVALUABLE ASSET TO HAVE TRUE spiritual friends and worthy adversaries to challenge the self-deceptions that skulk around at the fringes of our awareness. Fixations we prefer to ignore or that remain invisible to us, may be obvious to teachers, therapists, Dharma friends, worthy opponents and family members who are impaled by our faults and touched by our vulnerabilities, whether for kind or cruel reasons. Even those of us adept at self-reflection have nooks and crannies of fixation that are difficult to see when they are pillowed in a comfort zone of our own design. Sometimes these nooks are not mere crannies but gaping maws of self-centeredness, which come to light only in intimate relationship, when a serious interpersonal problem arises or some stealthy therapy lays bare a hidden hypocrisy.

So the caveat is this: while the suggestions and exercises that follow may facilitate the process of opening up, these self-help practices will be expedited if you find a genuine contemplative master, spiritual teacher, therapist or opponent or two to assist you. Having a psycho-spiritual ally is important in the calming down, tuning in and deepening phases of self-understanding, but still more valuable in seeing through the self-illusion. Seeing there is nothing to see, relaxing into groundlessness and letting authentic presence be, without subtly reifying the seeing or relaxing as a personal achievement, requires a deft, unsentimental touch. For virtually all of us, having a close relationship with a spiritual friend or contemplative maestro is crucial to seeing through the more subtle knots of self-deception. And on a nondual path like Dzogchen, it is indispensable to have a heart teacher to introduce and confirm recognition of naked presence as such.

Mindfulness

A calm and humble life will bring more happiness than the pursuit of success and the constant restlessness that comes with it.
— Albert Einstein

Appreciating that an unagitated mind is desirable is obvious enough, but living happy contentment forward is another matter. The foundation for any psychotherapy is the creation of a safe "holding environment" or relational home, allowing a person to feel secure enough to drop their shields and open up. Minimally of course, this involves a therapist or teacher manifesting a non-judgmental attitude. Likewise, the basis of meditation practice involves the creation of a calm state of mind able to let things arise as they will. As the Buddha taught, mindfulness is the basic practice for collecting an agitated, distracted mind. Whether we are anxious or depressed, beside ourself with rage or jealousy, numb with indifference or inflated with pride, mindful attention is an all-purpose medicine recalling the mind from being lost in its projections.

To develop this capability, Buddhist meditation elucidates Heidegger's rough outlining of meditative awareness, observing that mindfulness has two meditative aspects which accord to the Two Truths. The foundational aspect of *calm abiding* (*shamata*) collects the mind from its dispersion in proliferating thoughts. As this happens, *liberating insight* (*vipassana*) is unobstructed, and it becomes possible to see through self-world fixations.

As it stands, mindfulness meditation and its therapeutic applications are among the most researched topics in all Psychology. (Walsh & Shapiro, 2006) But it is important to note that what Psychology refers to as mindfulness is almost entirely limited to the practice of calm abiding. Properly speaking, there is no *practice* of liberating insight. Insight into and release of habit formations is not a meditation technique or anything that can be willfully done. Liberating insight only arises as we – at least momentarily – stop trying to *do* anything; thereby allowing projections to dissolve. Just as samsara means repetitively going round in circles, nirvana means the cessation of compulsive thinking. Contrary to much popular belief, the aim of Buddhist meditation is not to be calm. It is to calm down enough to unleash the liberating insight that cuts through the self-story. But in our hyper-stressed culture that is out of its mind in any number of ways, becoming calm is a nourishing goal in itself. In this context, calming meditation and mindfulness-based therapy are valuable forms of stress management even if they do not result in a more liberating insight.

As we know, mindfulness involves paying attention to what is actually happening rather than getting carried away by what we think is happening. Since the human condition includes dimensions of body, voice and mind, it is wise to address each of these in the service of calming the whole of our system. This is why sessions of meditation and therapy ordinarily begin with stilling the body by sitting down. With respect to voice, and the theyself tendency of dispersing our energy in idle speech, a meditator stops talking and a therapy client – ideally - collects their attention to address a meaningful concern rather than just rattling on. To settle a distracted mind, therapy addresses a specific topic while meditation focuses on a specific object of mindfulness, such as the breath, candle flame or mantra. Yoking the mind to a particular subject or object temporarily stills proliferating thoughts, thus creating an open space for attending to reactive patterns and creative impulses that operate under the threshold of consciousness. The distinction Lacan makes in regard to psychoanalysis, between empty speech and full speech, echoes the meditative distinction between mindless nattering and mindful speaking (right speech). A few mindfulness practices that help calm a monkey mind and relax somatic tensions follow.

Hitting the pause button

> Things are not as they appear. Nor are they otherwise.
> — *Lankavatara Sutra*

In calming down, everything depends on how wound up we are in the first place. If we are careening in a high intensity runaround, it may be impossible to get out of our head without using that head to talk ourself down. When compulsive thinking is so charged we can't slow it down, a more muscular intervention is required such as changing the channel, by intentionally distracting ourself. Taking a walk, run, bike ride or some other purely physical activity is useful for breaking a self-hypnotic spell and drawing down energy that has become fixated, thereby diluting the drama. It is a well-worn strategy for caregivers of upset babies and small children to deliberately distract them in order to interrupt a wailing jag or desperate grasping after some object.

When we are a bit less fraught, talking something out with a friend or sometimes merely complaining to a sincere listener, can help us dissipate charged energy and gather our wits. This is what many therapists, spiritual teachers, good friends and caregivers excel at: bringing a calm presence to bear on an agitated mind. As every therapist knows, sometimes even a brief phone call focused on nothing deeper than setting an appointment, may be enough to help an overwrought person step back from a precipice of panic. We can also talk ourself down, challenging catastrophizing thoughts with rational reflection.

Even though there is nothing special or in-depth about these common coping strategies, they can be remarkably effective when one is obsessively ruminating or emotionally flooding. That this kind of cognitive coping is a dominant therapeutic intervention for our age reflects both the privileged position of calculative thinking in our world and our estrangement from somatic-existential intelligence. Although conceptual reflection is helpful in talking one down from a crazed ledge, it is not yet awareness that attends to the energy flows/blockages of the emotional engine driving cognitive formations.

The critical turn of the Buddha's observation that the cause of suffering is grasping, and depth psychology's understanding that the cause of neurosis is repression, is the turning of attention around from its outer focus. And both agree this turn begins with hitting the pause button in compulsive thinking.

Coming to your senses: Calm abiding with support

To pay attention, that is our endless and proper work.
— *Mary Oliver*

With the mind proliferating thoughts charging emotions recharging thoughts, we fail to notice the space between a thought and emotion that allows us to make a skillful response rather than succumb to a knee-jerk reaction. To more ably access this transitional space, meditative awareness calms the mind by coming to our senses. In shifting attention from conceptual thinking to sensory awareness, the separation between mind and body is reduced. As awareness shifts from the airiness of mind to the earthiness of body, it reverses its outward cast, disengaging the aggregate of *form*. This shifts awareness from energizing a self-ground to opening to the groundless ground. Releasing psychic striving into transitional space opens a way to tap the natural resilience that wells up in uncontrived presence.

> stop making sense, stop making sense
> — *David Byrne*

Mindfulness meditation is traditionally taught as resting on four foundations: the body, feeling, mind/conceptual formations, and (as I discuss it) the nature of the mind. In a progressive mindfulness practice, the body is primary, followed by feeling, thoughts and the nature of thoughts. As an entry point, it is traditional and practical to begin with mindfulness of breathing. Since breath is the energetic link between mind and body, attuning to breathing is an easy and surprisingly powerful way to gather a dispersed mind and more fully inhabit the body. The following two exercises cultivate calm abiding with support. Support refers to reliance on objects. Here, the objects of mindfulness are physical sensations, beginning with the breath.

As mentioned earlier, in order to reverse the compulsive cascade of the I-process, it is necessary to let each of the five aggregates settle into their unelaborated nature. Through slowing the aggregating process down, we muster a presence of mind more able to see how it loses itself in projections.

Exercise 3

Whole body breathing

1. Begin by sitting comfortably either on a cushion or chair, with your spine in alignment. This position allows for the free flow of air into and out of your lungs all the way down to the belly, as well as allowing subtle energy to flow unimpeded through the channels. And close your eyes.
2. If your thoughts are galloping with you flopping in the saddle, you can corral them by counting breaths. Simply count "1" on the first exhale, "2" on the second, up to 10. Then repeating this 1 – 10 sequence again, and as many times as is necessary to slow the thoughts down to something closer to a trot. If your mind is not so out of control, this step can be dispensed with.

3. Bring your attention to the belly and the rising and falling of your diaphragm. Pay attention to the sensations of the moving belly and/or the passage of air at your nostrils. Remain focused on these sensations for some time, depending on how wound up you are – or how much you are enjoying the simplicity. The more agitated, the longer you should practice this one simple thing. In any case, feel free to linger with it, noticing the sensate richness in breathing and natural enjoyment in simply being alive.

4. Continue to settle more deeply into whole body breathing. Inhaling slowly, let the breath fill your lungs from the bottom of the belly up to the top, like water filling a vase. Exhaling, let the lungs empty completely. Pause briefly; remaining empty for a bit. And as the next inhale comes, again allow yourself to be filled slowly and completely, and then emptied in the same way. Fully inhabit your breath in its embodied rhythm.

5. Particularly if you are feeling stressed, and valuable in any case, you can add a visualization to the rhythm of respiration. On the inhale, imagine being filled with nourishing, fresh, clean, cooling air. And on the exhale, imagine being emptied of dirty, stale, hot, depleted air. Filling yourself with lightness and emptying yourself of heaviness and darkness. Practice this for at least 10 minutes, or as long as you like.

Exercise 4

Whole body sensing

1. Begin with calming your system through whole body breathing. Synchronizing your awareness with your breathing, consider that your breath is coursing through and renewing your whole body from head to toe. Carrying oxygen through the bloodstream to all your tissues, organs and bones, just as it carries away impurities and stale air. As this nourishment continues, and with your attention centered in your belly, let that awareness expand throughout the body. Fully inhabit your breath as your breath fully inhabits your body.

2. Then, with about 20% of your awareness remaining on the breath, direct the bulk of attention to the top of your head. Attuning closely to sensations, let awareness flow down from the crown of your head as if an egg had been broken on top. Feel for sensations as awareness moves down your forehead to your eyes and around the ears, relaxing any tensions you find along the way. Sensing down the nose and cheekbones to

the mouth and lips, around the jaw and its strong hinge below the ears, notice if you are doing any clenching. And then around to the back of the head and occipital lobes of the brain. Let awareness permeate your whole head, brain and its seven sense doors for awhile, letting awareness seep into your skin and muscles, including the smile muscles, allowing your face to relax.

3. At your own pace, move awareness into your neck and shoulders, tuning in to whatever tension you are holding there. Proceed down the arms to your hands, palms and fingers.

4. Returning attention to the neck and shoulders, linger there awhile before descending slowly down your spine, while radiating awareness around through the chest, heart and lungs. There, you may become more aware of your breathing and perhaps the beating of your heart. Continue to sense down your spine to the lower back and around to your digestive organs. Going slow and noticing where there are tensions or numb areas, let this inner sensing be an internal massage; continuing to relax places of tension in the back and abdomen.

5. Moving into your pelvis, feel your buttocks on the cushion or chair, and suffuse your sexual organs with awareness, opening to any holding around there while breathing into and relaxing the butt muscles. Descending into the thighs, continue sensing down the legs to knees and calves, ankles, feet and toes.

6. After this, allow your awareness to permeate your whole body from head to toe, all at once.

7. Within whole body sensing, now let your awareness be choiceless, freely moving to wherever it is drawn, touching what needs to be touched, attending to what calls your attention. As thoughts arise, let them come and go without following them, attending to sensations alone. Notice the vividness of sensory awareness and relax into that vitality. Enjoy the well-being intrinsic to sentience as such, unencumbered by complicated storylines.

Just sitting, just being

Of late I deeply devote myself to quiescence.
Nothing in the world concerns my mind.
The breeze from the pine woods blows my sash;
The mountain moon shines upon my harp.
You ask me to explain the reason of success and failure.
The fisherman's song goes deep into the river.

– Wang Wei

Even though there are hundreds of different therapies and countless meditative skillful means suited to all manner of people in all sorts of situations having all kinds of capacities, just sitting and breathing with full attention is sufficient for realizing total liberation. This is, after all, what the Buddha did under the Bodhi tree. Of course, in his favor he had spent the preceding seven years disciplining his body and mind, and in the process, presumably developed his capacity for non-distraction. Not to mention the preparation he apparently remembered and is said to have accomplished in previous lives. On this foundation, he then simply sat down and directed attention to his core life concern: *What is true?* Just sitting and breathing with this question in mind, but without relying on any particular method of meditation, he opened himself to experience as it flowed.

In simply being, he found, as will we, if we open nakedly to experience, the mind naturally calms down, tunes in and deepens. When a calm mind prepared to face the truth of human nature opens to that truth, resistances organically crumble. And in time, repressed habit formations spontaneously arise on the way to being released. So, just sitting calmly could be enough and would be enough to awaken, if we have the moxie to bear total openness. If not, it remains necessary to strengthen our capacity by becoming more able to tune in to ingrained fixations and bear greater intensities of genuine openness.

12

Tuning in

A purpose-driven life

What we are looking for is what is looking.
— *St. Francis of Assisi*

WHEN I WAS 20 YEARS OLD, I WORKED AS AN INTERN AT A RESIDENTIAL treatment center for seriously disturbed young adults.[13] As a fringe benefit, I received personal therapy as part of the job. During the course of that year, I found a profession that would give me a personally vital and professionally rewarding livelihood. Even better, the therapists at the center were avid meditators whose presence of mind inspired me to follow their lead. As it happened, the internship's end segued into a 2-week silent vipassana meditation retreat. This intensive introduced me to a way of self-attention that further inspired purpose for my life.

Although that first retreat showed me a life-changing way forward, that didn't mean I was able to let mindful awareness penetrate my repressive barriers to the depth of deeply rooted fixations. Even as meditation slowed my compulsive thinking, I unconsciously – and compulsively – adopted it as a defining characteristic of my purpose-driven life. Only years later did I realize I had undergone a religious conversion. I went from being spiritually bereft following my sister's death to being a devout Buddhist meditator. Like converts everywhere, I took the "good news" a bit far. Seeking peace of mind, I would sit on a cushion with closed eyes next to a kitchen timer that would ping when I was "done." Like a loaf of bread that had risen, I arose feeling lighter and with a sense of self-satisfaction.

Around that time, I came to live with a woman, let's call her Lena, with whom I had fallen in love, who was also a meditator. Our relationship was passionate in both loving and tedious ways. Its intensity was captured in an online blog written by a woman around the age I was back then, who had just moved in with her new boyfriend during the 2020 Coronavirus

---

13 The Country Place, outside Litchfield, Connecticut

pandemic for what at the time was an indefinite quarantine. She wrote, "After our first 24 hours together, things are going pretty well. We had sex twice and broke up three times." Living with Lena, one day we stumbled into an argument that was going nowhere but tight. Upset by it, I withdrew to our little meditation room to calm down. Concentrating as usual on my breath and sensations, the timer eventually pinged and I returned to Lena in the kitchen. Taking up the argument right where we left off, I continued bickering, realizing no benefit whatsoever from having meditated.

Feelingfulness

The thing about attaining a calm state, is that peace of mind fades as concentration wanes and fixations reassert themselves. Stilling the mind results in nothing more liberating than a brief vacation if it is not employed to uproot reactive patterns.

Attachment to tranquility is more of a problem in meditation than therapy; but is a pitfall in therapy to the extent client and therapist believe it is enough to temporarily feel better by being "held" within a supportive relationship. The limitation with maintaining a calm state is that it tends to remain dependent on its support, whether that support is an object of mindfulness, a yoga sequence, a recreational event, the companionship of a significant other, therapist, teacher or what have you. Once a becalmed mind dependent on a support loses that support, it will seek a replacement. Old habits of self-grounding quickly arise to fill the lack in the form of everyday obsessions. This is why, once we are able to dependably collect ourself, it is necessary to loosen our dependence on any particular support in order to more thoroughly dissolve our emotional dependency needs. Tuning in to underlying *wanting* gives us access to the aggregate of *feeling* (*vedana*) as mindfulness deepens into feelingfulness.

I just can't do this

The day arrived when the pain of remaining closed in a bud
was worse than the pain of opening.   — *Anais Nin*

Michael worked in the banking business for almost 40 years. Spending his days handling financial "instruments" and the numbers those instruments generated. He was a person overwhelmingly captivated by calculative thinking. This expressed itself as a hollowness in his relationships with his children and first wife, who divorced him for being emotionally distant. When he showed up in my office, his second wife was coming to a similar point of frustration, exhorting him to get into therapy. Michael was so out of touch with his feelings that he still could not clearly identify a feeling he was having after almost four months of weekly sessions. Any inquiry I made as to how he felt *on the inside* befuddled him as he visibly tensed.

Nevertheless, I sensed his emotional intelligence was bulging just below the surface. He was always quite anxious in therapy, which revealed itself on his freshly pressed shirts that began each session dry, but would be soaked with perspiration by the hour's end. Although opening himself was obviously daunting, Michael was intent on doing what he could to save his marriage. Banking on his high motivation, I persisted in inviting him to tune in to his liking or disliking of whatever topic we were discussing. Beginning with impersonal things, like the traffic or weather, and proceeding to his feelings about others, he eventually learned to identify his feelings in real time. This provided a foundation for my encouraging him to delve into his emotional reactions about himself.

Even though he was quite high functioning within the world of the they, it took him well over a year to get to a point where he could trust me and himself enough to emotionally crack the door of his self-shell. Although we addressed a number of topics during this time, the real therapy had little to do with what we discussed, but was about creating a relational space in which he might let down his guard. As another client once admitted upon reviewing his therapy after we had been working together for awhile, "I don't remember anything you said for the first six months. I was only interested in knowing if I mattered to you." Like Michael, this person was speaking of the need for a frightened mind to feel safe, supported and settled enough to tune in less guardedly.

Tuning in cannot be rushed. Otherwise, it can seem like a genuine opening when it is only a performance of self-disclosure operating in the service of self-defense. This occurs when a client reveals something they think the therapist wants to hear, whether to please the therapist or demonstrate that they are a good client. When this happens, talking *about* things functions as a defense against the vulnerability of actually *being with* what is talked about. Something similar occurs in meditation when we fixate on the peacefulness of a quiet mind. Tibetan folk wisdom compares a person who has heard and studied wisdom teachings but not yet taken them to heart, to a stone submerged in water. Even if a stone is immersed in water for a thousand years, it remains dry on the inside. Meditation fixated on tranquility is like being that (unbroken-open) stone.

But without fixating, as mental noise quiets awareness naturally expands into felt sensing, and we become aware of how we are micro-managing the flow of experience. Tuning in is what allows us to differentiate between the internalized voices and defensive reactions of the theyself and the wee, small voice of our inner sense.

Since it was so difficult for Michael to access his feelings, I did my best to meet him on his edge of openness. This meant neither pushing him to open nor ignoring that he was closed in a shell endangering the most important relationship in his life. In time, a vivid occasion arose for me to point this danger out. After struggling with his aversion against opening himself one session, he exclaimed with uncharacteristic feeling, "I can't do this, I just can't do this!" Which gave me pause, inspiring me to reply, "Michael, but you just now ARE doing it." Perplexed, he mumbled, "What do you mean?" "I mean just now in your exasperation: I can see you, I can feel you. You're not at all aloof or emotionally distant, but totally here, raw and open with me." Still perplexed, he grunted, "Huh?" So I continued, "Sure, you're frustrated; but that's the thing: you're not hiding that or pretending it's all OK when it's really and truly difficult... Right?" Him sitting in a stunned silence, I asked again, "Right?" Grudgingly, he replied, "Well, I guess." "You bet. This is a victory, your victory, Michael: you're being emotionally open and honest. That's what we've been working for and what Michelle (wife) has been missing and want-ing from you. And what you've been at loss to give her." A pregnant pause as he considered this. Then, "Well, yeah, I guess." To which I provocatively responded, "Only a 'guess?' Remember what you know to be true. What has Michelle been looking for from you?" Slowly, "Right; feeling." Warming and softening my voice as much as possible, I ask, "Do you guess or do you know that?" After a pause, "I know. That's it. But it's just so hard." "Sure it's hard, that's right. But isn't the price you pay for emotionally withdrawing hard on you in another, potentially far worse, way?" Another thoughtful pause. Then, "Yeah." And an extended pause as he seems to be taking this in. Then Michael looks up catching my eyes, something he rarely does. His unflinching eye contact displays a tuned in presence I had not seen before, as we share a moment of mutual recognition.

Tuning in is always a work-in-progress rather than a final victory. I could see, where he could not, that Michael's trying and failing and trying again is him courageously doing his work playing an edge of openness. The evidence of his struggle was the perspiration drenching his shirt each session. He was not comfortably disengaged in aloof withdrawal, but was showing up and tuning in as best he could. And while he may not have had much capacity at first for insights characteristic of depth therapy, he was absolutely in his depths, and slowly but surely going deeper.

Following this exchange, Michael became increasingly conscious of his self-story, revealing to both me and himself that he thought of himself as "not an emotional person." Eventually, he was able to see that this self-definition masked another belief that had been burdening him since we began: that he was not a good therapy client. He then connected this self-story to his belief he was not a good husband, father or financial professional. All of which turned out to be rooted in his belief that he was neither a good son nor good person. This interior badness seemed obvious to him, since his birth mother gave him up and his adoptive parents were often cool (mother) and critical (father). He made sense of this thinking there must be something bad or inadequate about him that he must police and keep under wraps. It was this negative sense of self laid down at an early age that energized his coping strategy of being emotionally distant, so as to not inadvertently repulse others and fail again in relationship. Ironically, it was precisely this self-defense that kept insuring his intimate failures.

And perhaps not ironically, but not obvious either, is how therapy itself contributed to Michael's inner conflict and sense of not being good enough. The purpose driving him in therapy, in both his and his wife's mind, was to change himself. When the common, and let's face it, essential, motivation for self-change, which is even more intense on a spiritual path, becomes heavy-handed, it exacerbates a self-aversion that paradoxically works to impede change. It can strengthen an inner conflict pitting the side of ourself that seeks change with the side that doesn't. Overlooking the fact that impermanence is the nature of the self, trying to change only blocks the flow that will inevitably change if it is left alone, and the stream of consciousness freed to move and evolve as it will.

Here again, since ingrained ways we think and feel about ourself seem true, how do we differentiate true feeling from a self-illusion? Teasing this apart involves opening to those implicit, perhaps contradictory, complexities we ignore in formulating the alibi of me.

One might think that a therapy exchange like this (and examples that follow) have little to do with a spiritual quest bent on enlightenment. That assumption could not be further from the truth. Therapy vignettes like this illustrate how working through resistance and deconstructing self-identity are facilitated in dialogue. A similar process occurs in meditation, usually involving an internal dialogue, but without it being guided or witnessed, thus remaining less visible. The key to both processes is to relax the striving for self-change and self-improvement, get out of our own way and open to the actual, all too human way we imperfectly are.

Choiceless awareness

There is freedom whether or not one realizes it.
— *Longchenpa*

We tell ourself we'd like to change, be easier on ourself or more confident; so who is stopping us? Practices of self-examination involve calling our own bluff. Freud famously declared that the fundamental rule in psychoanalysis is to freely associate: to open ourself without censoring what comes up. Together with his patients, he discovered that speaking freely exposes inner ambivalences which otherwise remain hidden. Bringing concealed and contradictory feelings to light challenges us to integrate the both/and of our mind rather than perpetuate the split of either/or thinking. Free association is a form of choiceless awareness that is also foundational to insight meditation. Having calmed the mind through one-pointed concentration, it becomes possible to then loosen that tight focus without being carried away by compulsive thinking. Since to be genuinely open is to be free, and to be free is to be untethered to a fixed sense of self, choiceless awareness allows fissures in the self-shell to widen.

For instance, Jackie entered therapy to deal with disturbing emotional reactions, mental images and psychic sensitivities that both frightened and intrigued her. Soon after settling into therapy, she began to remember incestuous incidents from her childhood. She eventually decided to share these memories with her mother, her perpetrating father and one of her three sisters. All three of whom disavowed any knowledge of this. Shortly thereafter, a second sister, who shared a bedroom with Jackie, admitted she remembered these incidents. Her third sister, who had completely separated from the family and lived abroad, refused to even talk about it. Even though Jackie had established herself as a confident, middle-aged professional, underneath her competent demeanor she suffered considerable self-doubt. Including questioning if she really was a victim of incest or if she just imagined it, as both her father and mother were suggesting.

As she was sifting through this, I listened to her with the most empathy and best suspension of belief and disbelief I could muster. But she came up against a wall and wanted to know, *Did I believe her?* It was clear that if I disbelieved her, she would feel that as a profound betrayal. Given the empathic resonance I had with her, I was predisposed to believe her story, since it had the ring of truth to it. But I also knew intuition could be fallible, and it was impossible for me to objectively confirm or disconfirm what she was remembering. More importantly, I felt her more important work was to discover for herself what was true. That my role was to help her tune in to her truth sense, independent of what anyone else, including me, thought.

When I didn't have a ready answer, her question abruptly hardened. She populated my silence with the conviction I did not believe her. For weeks we endured a fraught passage as I repeatedly reassured her I did not disbelieve her, even though I could not confirm her history. Jackie suffered severely during this period, thinking I was denying her reality. In taking things this way, those weeks were a kind of self-retraumatization for her. She vacillated between trusting and not trusting me, which mirrored her inner vacillation of self-trust. In being the object of her rage, I suffered as well, and was sorely tempted to capitulate with a confirmation of her memory. Resisting this temptation, I resolved to remain open to both her rage and my uncertainty.

Since her evolving story of herself now included a strong and disturbing storyline about me, I was somehow more embedded in her self-world, which afforded me inside leverage. This is the leverage psychoanalysis respects as a transference. Transference can make a fixation more workable insofar as it projects repressed feelings onto another person which can then be worked with in relationship, rather than suffered helplessly alone. It expands a person's predicament from being in a personal hell to being in a shared plight. Her suffering became our suffering.

Being able to stay afloat the two of us in a relational soup, I felt Jackie was strong enough for me to relax my power position in being the sole empath in the room. So, I asked her to tune in to me, and sense for herself if I was trustworthy and on her side. Fortunately, she was able to suspend her projection on me and shift her focus from a calculative, Did I or did I not believe her? to a less binary meditative way of being with me. It came as a welcome surprise to her, as she faced me, held my gaze and sensed in to me, that she could find no judgment in my being with her.

We met then, and often after that, in an intensified space of shared openness. In this, she allowed her childhood memories, current self-doubts and adult self-confidence to all commingle. It was within this spaciousness that she found herself more able to both trust me and trust being open to her inner complexities. It did not happen that her post-traumatic stress suddenly dissolved or that she became free from self-doubt. But she did become able to hold the whole catastrophe within a more inclusive, compassionate embrace.

Tuning in to *how* we are holding whatever it is we are holding, opens us to the grasping that constricts the mind in being for, against or in denial to whatever has happened, is happening or might happen. Whereas the aggregate of *form* corresponds to the earth element in Tibetan Buddhism, that of *feeling* corresponds to fire. Emotion flares up and runs hot or cold, feeding on some form as a fuel source. As emotional intelligence is quickened through felt awareness, enlightened intent flows more freely.

Attuning to enlightened intent

> In direct awareness, a deeper intention arises as the knowing
> that is present in each moment.   – *Ken McLeod*

All forms of self-inquiry governed by choiceless awareness share the ecological assumption that "unconscious process is a self-correcting system... [a psychic] ecosystem that will heal itself if left alone." As the cybernetic psychologist, Bradford Keeney, explains, this invites "therapists and clients [to] abandon their conscious, purposeful strategies of action and attend to the 'doing of nondoing' or *wu-wei* of the Taoist... Therapy thus becomes a context wherein a system finds its own adjustments." (1983, p.162) Tuning into the healing potential – enlightened intent – of existential intelligence employs meditative techniques as non-techniques.

Said in another way, it may not be apparent in either experience-near therapies or formal meditation practices that the method of tuning in and the wholeness being tuned in to are of the same nature. That which has been repressed is not other than a process of repressing continuing to happen just now. And that which is de-repressed, arising as an insight or felt shift, is not other than the process of de-repression, of being unconditionally present. Tuning in is the way a dispersed psyche withdraws its projections and accords with the evolutionary thrust toward well-being.

Felt attunement organically continues by opening to increasingly subtle levels of resistance. As projections withdraw in attuning to the process of projecting, self-defining narratives waver like the mirages they are. Withdrawing energy from fixations automatically gathers whatever aspects of experience have been split off. This in itself enables the integration of self-consciousness into the open nature of its unbound, contentless being. As Bugental puts it,

> Our truest nature is our contentless being. It has no habits or patterns, no neurosis or, for that matter, health. It is pure awareness, pure subjectivity. Subjectivity, bending in on itself, takes on form – content, perceptions, self-creation-by-awareness – which brings the expression of our beingness into the objective plane. Therapy, by fostering the client's loosening of compulsion or identity with the objective layer, releases the creative potential of his/her underlying subjectivity. This means that the real work of psychotherapy occurs beyond words, beyond logical-verbal understanding. (1981, p.423)

While some experience-near therapies recognize the inherently open nature of human being, it falls to nondual wisdom traditions to more confidently privilege contentless awareness and the potentiality of effortless liberation. Even so, both depth therapies and contemplative traditions agree that content-bound fixations can be cut through and openness enhanced by touching into the emotional holdings held in subtle energy.

Touching into subtle energy

Exercise 5

Mindfulness of feeling

Just as mindfully inhabiting the physical body helps muscles and soft connective tissues relax, mindfully attuning to the emotional body allows subtle energy to flow more smoothly.

1. Having calmed the mind through whole body breathing and sensing, breathe into the belly, tuning in to the flow of energy throughout your body. Notice whether you feel a distinct emotion, have mixed feelings, or a more diffuse, vague feeling-tone. Whatever your feeling, tune in to that and notice if you are holding your breath or otherwise managing the energetic flow. Without trying to change or prolong what is happening, open to your felt experience fully and completely.

2. Awareness has now engaged the second foundation of mindfulness, expanding to include feelings in addition to the breath and physical sensations. In touch with the vivacity of all this, let the flow of felt experiencing move as it will, tuning in to the richness of emotional presence. Depending on the time you have, linger in felt sensing for 10-15 minutes or longer.

Exercise 6

Touch and go[14]

Touch and go practice is especially useful when you find yourself on

---

14 This exercise is informed by the work of Karen Wegela, 1988.

an edge of overwhelm. It is a ready-to-hand way of befriending intensity, relating to vulnerability in a way that rocks the cradle as it were. The rhythmic play of touching in and letting go facilitates a workable relationship with emotional intensity.

1. Following from mindfulness of breathing, sensing and feeling, as you inhale, touch viscerally into your feelings; and as you exhale, intentionally let those feelings go. Synchronize the inhale with touching in and exhale with letting go.
2. Breathing in, tune in a bit more closely to your felt experience, as edgy or fuzzy as it may be. Breathing out, let that feeling go without going deeper into it or letting it become a big, perhaps overwhelming, deal. Simply and totally let the whole issue go its own way as you open a bit more to spacious awareness.
3. Inhaling and exhaling, touch in and let go as long as you like, with each breath opening and saturating the emotional body in awareness. Do this as long as it takes to feel that the intensity you are up against is manageable, letting things be as they are in a warm and spacious, but non-clingy, state of mind.

Exercise 7

Loving kindness

Treat yourself, your mind, with loving kindness.
If you are gentle with yourself, you will become gentle with others.
— *Lama Yeshe*

In order to more ably bear the intensity and insecurity that comes with greater openness, it is helpful to draw upon practices that actuate self-compassion. Invoking four Boundless Abodes (*Brahma viharas*), commonly referred to simply as the practice of the abode of *loving kindness*, these also include invocation of the abodes of *equanimity*, *compassion*, and *joyfulness*. As a feelingful enhancement of mindfulness, these intrinsically boundless qualities provide a heartfelt support for opening more bravely to groundlessness.[15]

---

15 This popular practice is discussed indepth by Sharon Salzberg (2004/1995), and covered by Tara Brach (2003), Karen Wegela (2009) and James Baraz & Shoshona Alexander (2012), among others.

1. Having settled the mind in a calm space and synchronizing breathing in the touch and go way, focus your inhale and exhale as going in and out from the heart region.

2. As you breathe, tune in to the center of your chest, repeating to yourself an aspiration on the order of, *May I be filled with* **equanimity** *and peace of mind. Rather than being run ragged by emotional reactions, may I be settled in the flow of things. May I be patient and at ease with myself and others.* As you think (and perhaps speak) these words, tune in to their felt meaning. Sitting like a mountain, stable and of the earth with the dignity of a Buddha, attune to a sense of unshakable equipoise. If it is present, spend some minutes deepening the sense of inner balance, letting equanimity become increasingly vivid. If a sense of inner balance is not present, then continue to empower the intention that it be so, by repeating the aspiration, which is already a self-blessing and sincere prayer.

3. Continue breathing from your heart, only now expand your intention to invoke a state of **loving kindness**. Thinking (or speaking) *May I be filled with loving kindness, saturated with gentleness toward myself and others. Rather than giving energy to criticism, blame or hatred of self or other, may my heart be open, gentle and kind. May I be suffused with true friendliness and selfless love.* As with equanimity, tune in to a palpable sense of kindliness and energize it with increasing vividness. Or, if you are just too anxious or angry to loosen your tensions, do your best to sincerely wish yourself well. Pray from your heart that you might be kinder and gentler with yourself and others.

4. Following this, expand the practice again by vivifying a sense of felt happiness with the aspiration, *May I be filled with* **boundless joy**. *Rather than getting captivated by feelings of inadequacy, jealousy or envy, may I feel contentment and delight just as I am. May I feel the full vivacity of being alive, and rest joyfully in the natural well-being of my heart of hearts. May I be filled with lightheartedness and saturated with a sense of gladness.* As with equanimity and loving kindness, indulge yourself in cultivating a greater and greater saturation of delight. If actual lightness of being is hard to find, then once again emphasize the blessing of your heartfelt wish to feel light and joyful and to have a buoyant sense of humor going forward.

5. Buoyed by a sense of equanimity, joy and love, continue by tuning in to an aspiration for **genuine compassion** for yourself and others. Praying, *May I be filled with real compassion; may I be free from indifference, selfishness and desperate clinging. May my heart be open, tender and receptive. May I feel true sympathy and heartfelt compassion for my own suffering and that of others. Furthermore, may I feel ruthless compassion for those who would harm or threaten me and others: may I be confident in setting clear, firm boundaries while leaving the door to my heart ajar.* Again, tuning in

to your pain and confusion, feel the felt richness of a compassionate response, perhaps also with a tinge of sadness for the whole thing. Breathe into and out of this heartfelt moisture, strengthening your capacity to be open and bear vulnerability. Still, if it is hard to feel genuine compassion at the moment, empower the aspiration to open your heart more fully going forward.

6. End the practice by resting in these divine abodes all together. Allowing the nourishment they bring to leave a deepening impression in your mindstream.

13

Deepening

To study Zen is to study the self

– Dogen

STUDYING THE SELF TO THE DEPTH OF A ZEN RECKONING INVOLVES looking into how we falsify experience. Examining how we are constru-ing reality interrupts the process of reification and disables projective identification, opening a window into the diaphanous nature of experience.

Deepening felt sensing

What is inside wants to know itself fully before it is born.
That's why it refuses to reveal itself.,
sure as you are that you need not slip down
that long branch of your body to the very root
and in the earth of your body hear the damp echo
of everything you have not touched
reflected in your voice, ...
Something you carried as a black weight for many years.
– David Whyte (1992, p.45)

It is my practice to occasionally go into solitary retreat in specially-con-structed cabins of total darkness. When someone unfamiliar with dark re-treat hears about this, they usually turn green. The purpose of these retreats is to apply advanced Dzogchen practices involving *natural light* – the intrinsic luminosity of being – in order to more deeply accord to lucid potentialities of enlightened intent. The foundation for these esoteric practices is the ca-pacity to abide in nondual presence. But since many people have little or no idea about such practices or presence, upon hearing I'll be spending a week or more alone in pitch darkness, shudder. They shudder not in awe of the luminous potentialities of nondual vision, but because, in imagining going into the dark themselves, they sense what would be waiting for them there. Fantasizing is not necessary, most people anticipate the danger they would be in right away. Captivated within divided consciousness, most everyone knows conditions of sensory deprivation will deprive them of external reference points, leaving them naked to themselves. Most people quickly intuit that such nakedness would evoke a return of what they have repressed. And indeed, when a mind lacks sufficient capacity to relax in its untethered, non-repressed nature, this is exactly what happens; as I well know.

Going into the wilderness or a meditation retreat (whether in light or dark) is a powerful way of leaving the comfort zone of the self-shell to develop our capacity for more ably bearing experience as such. The spiritual stalwart freely chooses this path, and sometimes against our will, life forces our hand. My marriage on the rocks in my late 30's, I discovered there were healthy and loving intimate relationships possible beyond the confusion, hostility and emotional distance I had become accustomed to with my wife. She and I agreed a separation was in order while we continued, yet again, to work on our relationship in couple counseling. But that earnest work could neither dissolve the chronic discord between us nor create a sympathetic rapport upon which to remake a happy home. It became obvious to me that divorce made sense. That was when I learned what Shakespeare meant in his line, "Hell hath no fury as a woman scorned."

The divorce became aggressive and bitter very fast, with lawyers getting involved and a custody battle engaged. I was a wreck. Under extreme stress, I find people often reactively manage their stress in one of two ways. Generally speaking, and using food as a primal example, we either stuff or starve ourselves. I found I was a starver. Not as far as anorexia, but I lost much of my appetite, would forget to eat or forget to finish eating; being so fraught with the whole catastrophe I lost enough weight friends began to notice. I had already gone back into individual therapy, which was enormously helpful. But I also wanted to ask Norbu Rinpoche, the wisest person I knew, how to handle the mess. I thought it would help that he knew my wife, who was also his student. His perfect dzogchen advice to me was "be Samantabhadra."[16] This was code instructing me to totally open myself and relax in non-reactive, lucid presence. It meant I should see through my projections just now! and rest in the ever-supple nature of mind. Even though I still treasure this heart advice, being now more able to apply it, at the time I couldn't pull it off. My dzogchen was not strong enough.

In therapy, I realized the hostility of the divorce was a natural karmic consequence, resulting from years of my wife and I giving energy to a hostile-dependent relationship. When I decided to breakup the dependency

---

16 Samantabhadra is the primordial Buddha. A symbol of the unconditional openness and non-hesitating responsiveness of authentic presence. He (she as Samantabhadri) is not a being, but symbolizes in human form, being as such.

part, that betrayed our tacit security arrangement, unleashing the wolves of the hostility part. Since there was no escape from going through the divorce, I had no choice but to be impaled by it, tooth and claw. In terrible situations like this, it becomes apparent that being able to briefly calm down and tune in is not enough to release deeper holdings. For me, the holding I was up against was intense fear and anger for what was happening to me, my children and even my furious wife. *Not this!* my mind cried. As I painfully rediscovered, in order to release the more stubborn roots of defensive reactions, it is necessary to more deeply open to those roots, and in untangling them bear being uprooted.

Through calming down and tuning in, the I-process of future-casting slows, so whatever we have been running from catches up with us. As this deepens, we are able to attend more carefully to emotionally grasping (*samjna*) and mentally fixating (*samskaras*). These aggregations loosen as we delve under storylines – *This should not be happening.* – to the repressed energy wells – *Not this!* – that fuel them. Again, the irony is that by not seeing the absolute truth that recognizes the fabricated nature of relative truth, we take the fabricated truth of our experience as being absolutely true. Without keen concentration, it is virtually impossible to disentangle an emotional perception from a mental formation (story of me), which is why I am considering them together. In terms of their elemental aspects, *emotional perception* corresponds to the water element, while the fabricating of *mental formations* is of the air element.

Since deepening immersion undercuts the grasping that holds the self-project together, this presents us with the challenge of facing our self-illusion, and in doing so, risk seeing that the face we see is not our own.

The two-foot drop

Not Revelation tis that waits, but our unfurnished eyes.
– Emily Dickinson

Reece was an imposing twenty-something tattooed biker, who initially saw me to deal with alcohol abuse. By his tough appearance, I wondered if he could be vulnerable enough to benefit from experience-near therapy. So, I brought up the question of his doing either an alcohol-specific treatment program or a cognitive-behavioral form of therapy I knew would make fewer emotional demands on him. He dismissed my concerns outright, and through three months of therapy showed he was well able to engage in depth inquiry. Since we focused primarily on his out-of-control drinking, he eventually looked into what was driving him to drink, touching into a gnawing sense of insecurity beneath his surface bravado. Around this time, he uncharacteristically missed two weeks of twice-weekly sessions. When he reappeared, striding into my office in his black leather jacket, pants and boots, the question of his absence loomed large.

As we settled into our chairs and I faced him, after a moment or two he met my gaze, and laughing in his endearing way volunteered, "I know, I know. I know what I need to do: the two-foot drop." Even though he did not look the part, he understood what depth work demanded if he was to deal with the roots of his addiction. I almost laughed as well, delighting in his astuteness. Although neither of us ever used these words before or talked about the process of therapy, we both knew what he meant. Reece meant that in order to effectively handle his compulsive drinking, he needed to deal with the deeper insecurity that was driving it. He knew – quite literally – he had to drop deeper into himself.

I still marvel at how a "two foot drop" perfectly measures the distance between the head and the center of the body. This recognition marked a turning point in his work, as his center of gravity shifted more to his heart and belly in daring greater emotional openness. As he risked more vulnerability, I noticed this and spoke to the courage he was showing in making the two foot drop, baring veiled fears, tenderness and confusion around the whole thing. It took him awhile to admit his openness was indeed courageous, since he had assumed bravery had to do with hardening the heart combat-style, something he was quite accomplished at. He came to see that it is a greater courage that neither defends nor attacks, but opens to quivering ambivalences and vulnerabilities head-on.

Invoking the actual

Are you live or on tape?

– *Jim Bugental*

Is your experience fresh and alive just now in the insecure and vibrant spectacle of life? Or, are you hurtling through time preoccupied with what is to come and replaying recordings of the past?

There are various skillful means that can disrupt complacency and facilitate entry into the here and now. Wilson Van Dusen recognized therapeutic conversations could either obscure or invoke the actual. In therapy, the actuality of lived experience is obscured when we talk around deeper thoughts and feelings, repeating the same old story without being touched anew by what we say. Van Dusen observed that "words and symbols are lifeless unless they choke, frighten, bring tears, or alert like the actually numinous." (1965, p.67) Invoking the actual marks the difference between a superficial talking about what is or has been or might yet be, and speaking from what actually is. For instance, the way a person carries themself as they walk, their tone of voice, eye contact and so on, reveals a good deal about how that person is actually being in the world, regardless of what they say about it. How a person sees and presents themself and how they show up may not be in accord. Attending to nonverbal behavior is a powerful way of bringing the divided actuality of the self into awareness, whether we are working with another person or examining ourself.

For example, Roberta was talking in therapy yet again about quitting her job and wondering if she should move away from the dangerous city in which she was living. Which in her neighborhood included daylight muggings. She had been complaining about this for over a year, struggling with whether leaving was a "cop-out" that would prevent her from becoming a stronger person through living under these threatening conditions. She wondered whether she deserved an easier life, and worried that she might not make new friends elsewhere. Depending on the day, we would discuss one of these concerns and I might either agree that it did make sense for her to move or reflect the question back to her, in which case she would usually confirm that it did. When she yet again asked, "Should I move?" I finally understood this was not her real question.

So, as she spoke I relaxed my focus on the content of her query. I then noticed she was keeled forward on the couch, hardly breathing as she spoke in a pressured way. Interrupting her train of thought, I observed, "You are holding your breath." She acknowledged this but didn't take it in. So I went further, "Roberta, you are on edge." That stopped her as she looked up and met my eyes. She looked a bit stunned, like a deer in headlights. So before she could recover and continue with her emotionally disconnected speech, I soldiered on, "What is your breath holding down?" With a groan, she said in trembling words, "I can't move. I'll have no one." At this point, her ambivalence of moving touched more deeply into her fear of being alone, and she was able to sit back and begin relating with her fear rather than merely talking about what to do about it.

Deepening immersion raises practical questions. Will the actual be evoked naturally or does it need to be invoked? Either way, are we able to tolerate what comes up?

One way or another, and whether in meditation or therapy, when stuff comes up that is an indication repressive barriers are loosening. As felt attunement deepens, energy flows more freely. And especially in sustained meditation, this facilitates the release of muscular tension and subtle holdings that can result in spontaneous postural realignments functioning like chiropractic micro-adjustments. Not uncommonly, a state of relaxed concentration is also accompanied by unusual shifts in breathing, as when the breath pauses upon exhalation for an extended time before the next inhale. Or, rapid bursts of exhalation from the belly may occur, which may be an involuntary form of the breath of fire practiced in Kundalini Yoga. I have found these odd kinds of breathing often function to draw energy down from the head into the belly, more deeply vivifying embodied presence. It can also happen that psychic sensitivity increases as breathing slows and deepens, lowering the pulse and blood pressure as a side effect, with awareness becoming lighter and more panoramic. These anomalous fluctuations reveal how subtle energy flows are facilitated naturally as the mind settles more surely into its unimpeded nature.

On the other hand, when a deepening process has been engaged but opening is resisted, pressure mounts. The challenge then is not that of tolerating openness, but of befriending the resistance to it.

Befriending resistance

Believe me, the hardest thing for a man to give up is that which he really doesn't want, after all.   *— Albert Camus*

Whether opening occurs as a gradual unfolding or we are rudely broken-open, light streams in; and depending on our readiness to face experience as it is, we find ourself either on a fertile threshold or in a real fix. This is the point where ego, to the extent it has not already been sufficiently decentered, panics, and like a vampire burned by daylight, recoils from the lightness of being. As awareness infiltrates deeper layers of the self structure, we are challenged that much more deeply to distinguish actual perceptions from projections. This entails working with resistance by playing the edge between ignoring our vulnerability and being overwhelmed by it. Respecting both our need for security and desire for freedom, suffering this both/and of the human predicament is the psychologically honest Way of dissolving our inner split.

Of the two general ways to play the edge of opening, gradual approaches (client-centered) are unquestionably the current standard of care in psychotherapy. Mindfulness meditation and spiritual paths in general likewise harness soft power in favoring a gradual approach. Although some spiritual practices, such as Rinzai Zen relational encounters or Tantric yogic practices that intensify the flow of subtle energy to blow through psychic blockages, aim to accelerate the process. These more vigorous approaches are not so interested in gradually working through resistances as in breaking through them. The *easy does it* approach I am presenting here proceeds gradually for the most part, by respecting that defenses are means of self-protection we have adopted for good reason. By gradually loosening inner knots, the tightness of a tangle is thawed out, teased apart and given leave to lift in its own time. Rather than a Zen slap, this is the way of a handshake.[17]

Playing the edge

All of us should try to learn before we die what we are running from, and to, and why.   – *James Thurber*

Whereas Reece's two-foot drop reflects an initiation into deeper work, the challenge of living greater openness forward remains. As self-awareness deepens, we find ourself up against increasingly subtle and perhaps more entrenched ways we protect ourself from the totality of authentic experiencing.

Magnolia, for instance, re-entered therapy to deal with a terrifying experience she had some years earlier during a course of bodywork. The bodywork she had done manipulated subtle energy flows in order to expedite the dissolving of psychic blockages. It worked rather too well. While on the table one session, Maggie experienced an intense disembodied opening, flooding her with terror and disorientation leaving her reeling for weeks afterward. Her opening was a true spiritual emergency which left her frightened of further opening, even as she sought it. She managed her anxiety by keeping things in order and being a much appreciated helper to others. Coping in this, her habitual way, she rehabilitated a self-world illusion that existence was manageable and under control. But this self and world control, bolstered by others' love and validation of her, did not fool her unsettled inner sense that kept longing for greater authenticity.

By the time she saw me, she was a committed meditator and spiritual seeker who felt the need for an in-depth therapy relationship to facilitate her opening. We agreed it was necessary to modulate her openness in order to better tolerate and integrate what came up. At her initiation, we began each session sitting briefly in silence as a preparation for her to touch more deeply inward. Soon enough, things did get touchy.

Like the two foot drop, touchy well describes what deepening immersion feels like. The challenge for Maggie was not to ambitiously go deeper, since deeper was near at hand. Rather, her work was to befriend touchiness by giving it room to breathe and speak or remain silent as it was inclined. This required going slow, following the Chinese folk maxim to *cross the riv-*

---

17 "Handshake" is another favored metaphor of Tsoknyi Rinpoche's, conveying a befriending approach to self-reckoning.

er by feeling for the stones. In Maggie's process of deepening, feeling for the stones entailed attending to her resistance against being fully present. This showed up in her being overly agreeable or wanting herself and me to do therapy in an orderly, hopefully perfect, way. At times, she would get upset if she thought I was withholding validation from her by not mirroring back her therapeutic competence. These were ideal occasions to observe the perfectionist expectations she was, in spite of herself, continuing to empower. Looking into this while warming up to the emotional intensity around it, Maggie found herself increasingly able to play the edge of her fear of going crazy by opening too much. Finding she could access deeper immersion, she was able to handle increasing intensities of feeling. This in turn challenged her to more deeply release on the story she was telling herself about being unable to bear such openness.

Befriending resistance involves noticing how we are managing, narrating or otherwise shrinking experience to fit. Both meditation and experience-near therapy focus less on the self-story that informs a defensive reaction than on the emotional need for defensiveness. Focusing on the resistance to full presence rather than whatever it is that is being resisted, cuts under the *story of me*, opening to the core dilemma of trying to defend ourself from our experience.

Deconstructing self

> Meditative techniques decondition the mind from its tendency to secure itself by circling in familiar ruts, in this way enabling its freedom to become anything. Such a mind is unborn and uncreated, yet it cannot real-ize this as long as it consciously or unconsciously understands its fundamental task as making itself real or finding some safe home.
>
> *– David Loy*

As emotional reactions and mental fixations unwind, aggregated I-functions become less entangled as the grasping that binds them together loosens. In being less bound, they function more autonomously and less like a mob. Ego disentangling is expedited by de-constructing the narratives that glue *me* together.

For instance, Rhonda had a good deal of insight into herself, understanding how her aloof mother, critical father and punishing older brother created a childhood environment which undermined her self-confidence, leaving her feeling chronically unsure of herself. Even though she had a good relationship with a life partner and was a licensed therapist with an Ivy League education, she worked for an insurance company in a position below her capability. And even though she was well aware of this, bored with her job and frustrated by a less-capable manager who would criticize her for his own failings, she was too insecure to leave the security her position provided. At a point when she was once again bemoaning this situation and her own timidity in it, a question that had been forming in my mind for some months clarified. I wondered out loud if she was indulging in feeling sorry for herself, thereby keeping herself stuck and depressed.

To that, she exclaimed in a tone of desperation, "But that is the base of my insecurity. If I let that go of that, what will I have!?" As we sat there, stunned into silence by what she had just said, a bemusement bubbled up in me. She inadvertently "let the cat out of the bag." Within the field of good humor that existed between us, she saw this, saw that I saw it, and could not suppress a furtive smirk. Feeling she was ripe for deepening this insight, I mused, "What would happen if you were to let that go? Just for a minute here. How would it be without that base?" She took a moment considering my challenge. Then apparently did let go, uttering an "oh." And with a smile creeping across her face, "That isn't so bad. That's nice." So I asked, "What's nice?" "Ah, that. I don't know. I feel lighter, better." "You mean without a base?" "Yeah," she said. And then, "That's the Buddhist thing, right? Emptiness?" "Well, maybe it is" I replied, wondering out loud, "A kind of spaciousness?" Then with softer eyes and light seeming to come off her, she quietly confirmed, "Yeah." I continued, pressing my advantage, "So how would it be to let this empty space be?" We then spent some moments silently sharing spacious awareness.

This deepening marked the beginning of a new dimension of experiencing for her. From then on, she was more able to observe, and increasingly release, how she grounded herself by identifying as twitchy, insecure Rhonda. Seeing herself more clearly and befriending her pain without taking it on, allowed her to be more at ease in her skin. In terms of the aggregates, this passage involved working with her *conscious* and *unconscious* (*vijnana*) self-stories through deepening her immersion in the emotional soup energizing those stories. Even better, her capacity for deeper settledness allowed her to linger longer at times in the contentment of simple openness. Both therapy and mindfulness meditation may be inclined to overlook the space that opens when an issue resolves or tension releases, moving on to the next issue or object of mindfulness. But when these practices are able to privilege non-conceptual awareness, authentic presence is given the opportunity to deepen.

Befriending resistance and accepting that experience as it is is the place to be, we are able to recognize the freedom and meaningfulness inherent in whatever is already happening. Thus, the whole project of striving for meaning, self-improvement and liberation becomes vaguely suspicious. Recognizing our Reality is not as Real as it seems inclines us toward a less gradual, more direct way of release through accelerated yogic methods and non-gradual teachings. But whether we take it slow and easy or take a deep, direct dive into The Mystery, liberation is expedited by letting opened-up-ness more thoroughly permeate our system. Until we are free of wanting and self-grounding no longer holds an appeal, it is necessary to play the edge of wanting and not wanting to be free.

Transmuting emotion

> Things falling apart is a kind of testing and also a kind of heal-
> ing. We think that the point is to pass the test or to overcome
> the problem, but the truth is things don't really get solved.
> They come together and they fall apart. Then they come to-
> gether again and fall apart again. It's just like that. The healing
> comes from letting there be room for all of this to happen:
> room for grief, for relief, for misery, for joy.
>
> *— Pema Chodron*

Since my dzogchen wasn't working in the hell realm of my divorce, I downshifted to basic mindfulness practice. And while that did work, afford-ing me a measure of relief, the gradualness of its method could not match the emotional intensity or mental chaos of the divorce storm. I needed more help, therapy notwithstanding, to metabolize the severity of my turmoil. So, I began the practice of *tonglen* in earnest. In terms of directness, I consider tonglen to lie somewhere between mindfulness and nondual paths such as Dzogchen.

Unlike mindfulness meditation, which bides its time in choiceless aware-ness, tonglen is choiceful in deepening the practice of *touch and go*. Literally translated as "giving and taking," tonglen involves not merely touching, but diving into the emotional churn underneath mental stories; and then giving away whatever limited security and satisfaction those self-stories give us. This practice actuates emotional intelligence by transmuting defensive reactions into compassionate responses, which I was in dire need of at the time. Being at risk of either hating the mother of my children or feeling sorry for myself and my kids to the point of hating myself into a depression, or both. Along with my therapy, I credit tonglen practice in helping me get through that dark night.

During the worst of that period, I was practicing tonglen every chance

I had. And since I happened to be teaching my usual graduate course in Existential Therapy, I wound up not only sharing it with my students, but making it a mainstay of the course. Apparently, the value I found in it resonated with a number of those students, who asked to continue with it when the course ended. That marked the beginning of my Dharma teaching, as an intent sangha (spiritual community) formed around me in the service of heart-opening.

Without a doubt, moment-to-moment mindfulness will eventually tame the striving to get somewhere other than here. But when we are in especially difficult situations, it is advantageous to accelerate this process to meet the more evocative conditions. And even when life is easy, rather than struggling with sleepiness and distraction while waiting for core fixations to arise in their own time, we can go looking for trouble, tonglen-style. As traditionally taught, giving and taking is a Mahayana-class practice oriented toward helping others rather than oneself. It involves both mentally and physically giving away good stuff we would like to keep, such as love, happiness, money and pleasure, while taking on bad stuff we would like to be rid of, such as pain, despair, poverty and fear. The principle behind this counter-intuitive practice is to reverse ego-grasping and aversion. Tonglen accomplishes this by transmuting self-centeredness into other-centeredness, diminishing defensiveness through invoking empathy and awakening compassion. However, given the severity of divided selfhood in our world, I have found tonglen is more effective if it begins not by focusing on the other, but by tending first to the otherness within ourself.

Exercise 8

Tonglen: Yoga of transmutation

Since there are a several descriptions of tonglen practice readily available,[18] I will only outline the basics of this practice here as I have modified them to contemporary needs. The first of two phases is devoted to practicing for oneself. The second extends this (more traditionally) to others.

1. **Phase One:** Having settled your mind in a calm space, focus on breathing in and out from the heart. Consider that the purpose of the practice is to transform yourself. The attitude is this: if something or someone needs to change, let it be me.

18 See Chodron and Brach in the *Further resources* section.

2. As you inhale, imagine breathing in heavy, dark, polluted air, like filthy smoke. As you exhale, send out light, clean, purified air, like a sparkling spring day. Spend awhile synchronizing your breathing with this visualization until your system readily accepts taking in dirty, foul air and giving out nourishing fresh. Emphasize both phases as equally as possible.

3. Then, tune in to whatever is currently difficult, painful or unwanted in your life. As you tune in, breathe it in. Feel in under the storylines about it to the bodily felt sense of the thing. Exhaling, let it go. Inhaling, breathe it more deeply in, tuning in to the worst of it. Follow the pain to its core, tuning deeper in to how it is weighing on you, how it is holding you/how you are holding it. Do this on repeated in-breaths until you feel you are palpably in touch with the whole of it, or as much as you can stand. Exhaling, release on the whole of it as much as possible; following your breath out into the vastness of space. Continuing on the inhales deepening to the bone, to the dark core of the thing, taking the pain, leaving nothing out. Exhaling, let the pain go. Every little bit. Empty yourself completely of whatever and however you're holding.

4. Continue in this rhythm as long as it takes to feel the full intensity of whatever is bothering you, breathing it all in.

5. Then, consider what strengths you need in order to better manage or befriend this mess. Perhaps you need some loving kindness or self-compassion, equanimity or a sense of humor. Maybe patience would be helpful, or courage, self-respect or self-forgiveness. Whatever comes to mind that you need in order to handle the pain, exhale expanding that quality.

6. Inhale as before and exhale this or these nourishing qualities, repeating the taking and giving until your energy flows unimpeded, your tensions soften and your mind lightens.

7. Letting yourself completely off the hook, emphasize the letting go exhale. Accompany your out-breath into spacious awareness.

8. **Phase Two**: If you wish to practice for others, while resting in spacious awareness, bring to mind the other(s), feeling into their energy and predicament. Sensing into them, inhale their pain along with your own. Exhaling, radiate release, compassion, courage, equanimity, whatever you feel would be helpful, through you to them.

9. This can be extended by breathing in the suffering of people you do not know who suffer in a similar way, and exhaling whatever quality you all can benefit from.

10. More powerful still, is breathing in the pain and confusion of an adversary or someone you do not like or who does not like you; someone who has offended, betrayed or otherwise hurt you. Breathe in the poison of their hatred, confusion or possessiveness, taking it in as much as

you can. Exhaling, let yourself be the change, regardless of what they did, metabolizing the poison into ultimate medicine by letting go of the pain, blame, vengeance and hard-heartedness you harbor because of them. Kindly send out love, forgiveness, equanimity or a prayer that they be released from their confusion, and the aggression, indifference or desperate clinging they suffer because of that.

11. End by emphasizing the exhale and letting go into the vastness of space.

14

Seeing

To study the self is to see through the self.

— Dogen

ALTHOUGH WE MAY RECOGNIZE THE TRUTH OF IMPERMANENCE AND intellectually accept the truth that there is no enduring self, until we know these truths without a doubt, we do not completely believe them. Even as deepening self-inquiry loosens psychic knots and leads to their dissolving, it does not necessarily dissolve the knot-maker. Deepened felt sensing is not yet a liberating that liberates the wanting to be liberated.

Beyond the search for meaning

The more comprehensive the meaning,
the less comprehensible it is.

— Viktor Frankl

Mustering the courage to relate to the raw actuality of experience as well as the humility to recognize habits of self-deception takes us as far as psychological work can take us. Through loosening the most troublesome fixations, we strengthen our capacity for tolerating openness, leaving us more free and self-possessed rather than they-possessed. This psychological sanity brings us to the threshold of a more basic sanity that emerges as we take the further step of seeing through the self-illusion.

However, this further step is not really a step, but more like missing a step, as when we find ourself moving through space without a ground. When we miss a step, whether walking down stairs or on uneven ground, there is a moment of groundlessness. And even once our foot touches down again, there are some residual moments of lightheadedness. Having missed a step, we are a bit dizzy at having found ourself momentarily aloft. Seeing through the self-illusion is like this.

Finding ourself in the space between thoughts – that are otherwise busy narrating the story of our life – is conducive for seeing through self-world projections to the projector. Not only might we see that the Great Oz is actually an embarrassed little man behind a curtain, but that that small, frightened self is no self at all. Seeing this, if only for a moment, it dawns on us there is no self to improve and no personal meaning to search for. Releasing on the search for meaning, which is similar to the psychological search for authenticity, momentarily liberates projects of both self-improvement and -realization. In moments of contentless awareness, we are free from any sort of narrative bypassing. This cessation is where psychological understanding and spiritual liberation part ways.

As we have been considering, psychology focuses on mental-emotional states while contemplative spirituality is oriented toward the contentless nature of psychic states. Which is why, as a preparation for seeing through the self-illusion, meditation instructions direct practitioners to notice the gaps between thoughts. Observing that the stream of consciousness with which we identify is not seamless but like a video clip made up of successive frames, undermines the solidity of *me*.

Noticing the gaps within our mindstream allows us to distinguish between thought and non-thought/self and non-self. Before slowing the mind down and seeing these gaps, we assume the mind/self is a seamless continuity, confirming the apparent ground(s) of our Reality. But upon noticing the gaps, we discover that thoughts/feelings/sensations and non-thought/-feeling/-sensation oscillate one after the other in an ephemeral cascade. Sutra-based Buddhism understands this difference between something and nothing as that between conditioned (cloud) formations of samsara and the unconditioned, unformulated space of nirvana. As mentioned earlier, this ontological difference is still a conceptual formulation. It is not yet the recognition that sees that both thinking and (the gaps of) non-thinking are of the same nature. There is still the radical discovery to be made that experiences, experiencing and the experiencer are all essentially empty-open, of the nature of space, being themselves in gaps and of gaps.

> When verbal assertions cease, named things are in repose; and the ceasing to function of discursive thought is ultimate serenity.
> — *Chandrakirti*

As an ardent meditator traveling around North America to the few vipassana retreats being offered in 1976, I hitchhiked from Ohio to British Columbia, where Ruth Denison was leading a 10-day retreat. That retreat was quite evocative for me, as toward its end I opened to a vein of terror which left me trembling. When a group meditation session ended, I could walk the terror off; but upon returning to the cushion it would engulf me again. Following the final meditation period one evening, I unsteadily approached Ruth and told her what was happening. As yogins filed out of the hall wrapped in meditation shawls against the autumn chill, she invited me to come to the front of the hall and sit with her.

With closed eyes, we sat facing each other in the dimly lit old barn that had been repurposed into a meditation hall. We sat for some time as cold fear broke out again over me. In her steady presence, I was able to open more completely to it and the distance between me and it collapsed. As this separation dissolved and I swam in the flux of naked experience, it became obvious that what I was experiencing as *my* terror was an arising that was neither me nor an actual outer threat, but a strong undertow in my stream of consciousness. Seeing the insubstantiality of both me and it, the tension of the whole thing abruptly lifted. This recognition, which went deeper than any cognitive insight, released me into an ecstatic clarity having the texture of bliss-saturated well-being. I knew myself in a way I had not known before. Even though it was also clear I had, somewhere in the back of my mind, always known this, my true nature. Resting in awareness as such, I continued to sit in silence, enjoying the releasement. So it surprised me when Ruth quietly spoke, "its beautiful, isn't it?"

Only later was I able to verify that not only was Ruth a rare and relationally marvelous teacher, but that the kind of subtle attunement she shared with me is something that can be enhanced through contemplative experience. While empathic resonance can be overwhelming for a "gentle soul," hence the development of defense mechanisms to buffer vulnerability, seeing the insubstantial nature of that gentleness frees the sense of vulnerability that comes from identifying with it. Seeing there is no distinct I to defend and nothing to lose, gives vulnerability wings. Fear morphs into awakened heart.

In that breakthrough glimpse with Ruth, my system momentarily let go of how it/I was holding itself/myself. As Jim observed, inner seeing is not *an* insight, but is awareness aware from within itself: seeing/being/awareness as such. The *withiness* of naked awareness is all-inclusive. It is beyond free association, active imagination, inward searching, focusing, mindfulness, or akin forms of self-inquiry that seek to go deeper into this or that experience. Unconditional presence is seeing without seeking. With the collapse of the subject/object split, there is nothing to search for, defend or promote. The intrinsic wakefulness of awareness reveals the stream of consciousness to be an uncreated and unceasing display; a self-perfected wonderment unimpaired by having problems and unimproved by finding solutions.

Seeing through the self-illusion into the spacious nature of the consciousness (*vijnana*) that constructs it, reveals that the elemental nature of consciousness is space. In addition to the usual four elements, Tibetan Buddhism recognizes a fifth element: *space*.[19] Even though a moment of vision into the spacious nature of experience is a non-gradual recognition of authentic presence, the meditative preparation that increases our receptivity to nondual vision occurs gradually moment by moment, day after day.

Since recognizing the nature of mind is a seeing that sees there is nothing to see, it is a recognition of both the groundlessness and timelessness of now. Here, the hope and fear arising from wanting lose their support and dissipate like rising mist. Just this is the liberation the Buddha realized. Unlike the Buddha however, who was able to fully embody nondual vision going forward, a glimpse of authentic presence is just that and will pass. Which is why it is necessary to practice the letting go of mindstates and seeing over and over again the dreamlike nature of those states.

Letting go: Dying before you die

To let go and become groundless is to realize that that hole of feeling incomplete is what [truly] grounds me: because it allows me to be grounded in the totality of interdependent relations.   — *David Loy*

When we notice we are fixated on something or other, the practice of letting go is to feel the burn and drop it like a hot coal. When we are on the threshold of doing so, it can feel like we are losing our mind (ground) and tremble at the threat of non-existence. Which is what I was up against in the Canadian vipassana retreat. A helpful aphorism here, which has been attributed variously to Socrates, Mohammed, Zen masters, Christian mystics and Krishnamurti is, *If you die before you die, then when you die, you do not die.* This wisdom nugget has been a refuge for me when I've been up against an especially deep-seated fixation, tempted to either numb, distract or blame myself for the suffering breaking me open. Letting go of a deeply rooted habit formation can elicit the sense *I* am dying. Which is just about right, since habit formations are what keep self-identity alive.

The realization that dawns as self-ground gives way and we find ourself in freefall, is that falling is not a problem, since within spacious awareness there is no ground to crash into. With this recognition – like a hawk catching

---

19 Sometimes this element is translated as "ether," as it is in other mystical traditions. While this offers an appropriate echo in the word ethereality, it is both archaic and misleading in being suggestive of a gas, which belongs to the element air rather than the no thing of elemental space.

an updraft above a chasm – falling transforms into soaring. Trembling as we open to our terror, it is worth reminding ourself that it is okay to die. This self-reassuring works like a small bird flapping its wings like mad against the gravity, in our case, of a habitual self-ground. With more practice dying into a life free of fixating, our capacity expands into the broad wings of a hawk, and we are able to delight in groundlessness, soaring on thermals, seeing far. As Trungpa put it,

> Letting go is connected with letting go of any vestiges of doubt or hesitation or embarrassment about being you as you are. You have to relax with yourself in order to...discover a bank of self-existing energy that is always available to you.... It is the energy of basic goodness. (1984, p.78-84)

Letting go of the self-story that binds our energy, we drop more surely into the current of enlightened intent. Instead of being inside the meanings we make, we become more able to tolerate The Mystery through which meaning emerges, pirouettes and exits sight unseen. To the degree we are able to consciously die before we physically die, when death arrives, to that degree there will be no separate self that dies as bodily elements disperse and brainwaves flatline. It will then be evident, that in dying, what is dying is not me, but only transient processes I once mistook for myself. At this point, it becomes apparent that what the self-sense feels as vulnerability, naked awareness revels in as inviolability.

In order to more confidently let go, it is helpful to have glimpsed the luminous well-being inherent to unfabricated presence. Being familiar with spacious awareness allows us to more easily let go into it.

Exercise 9

Exhaling into spacious awareness

Among my favorite letting go practices is one based on a further modification I made to tonglen, emphasizing the dissolution of self-referencing.

1. Begin with the practice of tonglen (Exercise #8), fully inhabiting your sensory and felt awareness by inhaling whatever in your experience is difficult or unwanted. This exercise works best if the breathing-in goes to the core of your sense of wanting, pervading your chest and belly.

Exhale tonglen-style, letting whatever you are holding go.

2. When you are in sync with the inhale-exhale rhythm, shift the balance of your attention to emphasize the letting go of the exhale. Breathing-out, completely exhale whatever you are aware of, whether it is delight, misery or some variety of indifference. Rather than focusing on what you are releasing, focus on releasing itself. The idea is not to send out anything positive or nourishing as it is in traditional tonglen, but to emphasize the mere letting go. Exhaling into space, empty yourself of inner holdings, preoccupations and reference points of all kinds.

3. Continue this emptying rhythmically for a few out-breaths.

4. Then go a step further. Upon exhaling, remain empty for a bit, resting in the vastness of space. Linger in spacious awareness, allowing the next in-breath to come when it will.

5. Upon inhaling completely, when the exhale goes, let every little thing go without remainder. Let whatever is on your mind evaporate into trackless space as your consciousness vanishes along with it.

6. Empty and open, rest in contentless awareness. In mingling your awareness with space, notice the ineffable nature of simply being.

7. Patiently wait for the next inhale, and after it arrives, also calmly wait until it comes time to exhale. Upon exhaling, continue resting and enjoying the spacious wakefulness without following any thoughts that arise.

8. Rest easy in open awareness without periphery or center.

9. At first, it is good to do this practice briefly, ending with a clear recognition of spacious awareness before it has a chance to be obscured by proliferating thoughts. And then, repeat it many times in short shots, treating yourself to many glimpses without trying to hold onto them.

The open heart sutra

The great mystery of being is that all experience, thoughts, feelings, and sensations arise from nothing and dissolve into nothing.
                                                                    – *Ken McLeod*

The short, sweet *Heart Sutra* provides a template for seeing through the self-reification process that is construed through the aggregation of sensing, feeling and thinking. As a human scientific inquiry, the Heart Sutra can be read as a single-subject research study conducted by an astute introspective investigator. Avalokitesvara looked deeply into the substance of each constituent of his self-experience, and reported his findings in the sutra, revealing the quintessence (heart) of self-existence. It begins with its radical conclusion.

> When the Bodhisattva Avalokitesvara engaged in deep self-inquiry,
> he found that the five aggregates were non-existent, thus
> securing his liberation from all wanting and suffering.

With the keen eye of a contemplative adept, Avalokita looked into the self-aggregates one by one and made his famous declaration:

> Form does not differ from emptiness, nor does emptiness differ
> from form. Form is the same as emptiness, emptiness is the
> same as form.

While this is the classic line conveying the heart of the sutra, Avalokitesvara did not stop there.

> The same is true of feeling, emotional perception, mental
> formations, and consciousness in relation to emptiness.

These findings proclaim the insubstantial nature of all psychic experience. Even though each constituent seems real, when deeply looked into, not one can be found.

Nevertheless, and this strikes to the core of The Mystery: even though sensations, feelings and concepts cannot be found, they continue to arise. When this astonishing paradox is directly experienced, and not just intellectually understood, we are liberated from any *wanting* that comes with identifying as a separate self. Seeing through dualistic projections and discovering that self-world fixations are but flimsy fabrications, a shift from a paranoid sense of self to a compassionate sense of being-oneself occurs. Although the recognition of non-self is considered wisdom in Buddhist thought, its essential openness radiates unconditional love. It is completely fitting that Avalokita, the main Bodhisattva of compassion in Buddhism, delivers this open heart sutra. The truest compassion, free from both closed-heartedness and sentimental clinging, is an expression of the ground-penetrating radar of incisive cognizance (*prajna*).

As always in Buddhism, the *emptiness is form* (*feeling, thinking...*) assertion is neither to be passively accepted as scriptural authority nor as scientific fact. It is the original koan thrown down as a linchpin enigma for those who dare to look into it, and by looking into it, see if the Buddha and Avalokitesvara got it right and the liberating paradox is indeed true. This inquiry can proceed methodically, one step at a time, as Avalokitesvara observes, or, since the I-process cascades so fast, it can proceed on the fly by examining whatever sensation, feeling or thought happens to be dominant in the moment.

Exercise 10

Seeing through the self-illusion

> Authenticity amounts to the resolution of the subject-object split, the self-world dichotomy. As one approaches the stage of letting go to the suchness of being without striving against it, one is attaining to full authenticity.   — *Jim Bugental*

1. Begin by settling into a calm state. Then, consider the components of self-experience – sensations, feelings and thoughts – by noticing which of these is prominent just now.
2. If thinking is prominent, look into the thought. ***Look into where the thought arises from, where it resides, and where it goes.*** Looking into its *source*, notice how thought arises from nowhere. If you think you can identify a somewhere, either inside or outside, notice that this location is itself located in a locating thought. So look into the source of this locating-thought. Finding no source, another thought may arise, such as, "I can find no source."
3. Whenever the next thought arises, look into where that thought *resides*. As you try to locate it in the present moment, you may find it too cannot be found. Again, if you think you can find it, notice where this finding-thought is. And if you think you've found a finding-thought of the original thought, see if you can find where the finding-thought that has found the original thought is to be found. Even though a thought cannot be definitively found in the present moment, notice the wakeful awareness of its unfindability.
4. Then, notice the next thought arising, such as, "I can find no source." Or, "Although a thought cannot be located, I am conscious of it, so thought is the stuff of consciousness." Look to see where this thought *goes*. Not being able to find where it goes, see the nature of your looking but not finding. See that thinking is emptiness, emptiness thinks.
5. Proceed in the same way when a sensation is prominent. Look to see from where it comes from, where it is, and where it goes. Observe that finding no concrete source, location or destination for a sensation dissolves the grounds of a perceiver, but does not block the flow of perceptivity. Sensation is emptiness, emptiness senses.
6. And do the same threefold inquiry with a feeling. Even though the source of a feeling cannot be found, notice how quickly thinking can fabricate one. For example, "I am angry...because Joe insulted me,...the

jerk." Note that this feeling-laden conclusion involves perceiving, thinking and judging, not only feeling. Embellished by judging and thinking, a feeling aggregates, becomes appropriated as *mine* and sticks to us like gum to a shoe. This is the I-process in the making. Looking into where an emotion resides in the present and where it goes in the future, it once again becomes impossible to locate or track. It becomes obvious that emotion is empty, yet emptiness emotes.

7. Seeing the no-thingness of experience momentarily interrupts the process of reification. As attention shifts from coming from an inner self focusing on outer objects to coming from nowhere and everywhere, non-binding, nondualistic vision reveals itself to be simultaneously personally embodied and impersonally spacious.

8. Seeing this, simply relax into panoramic awareness.

9. And when the next feeling, sensation or thought arises, allow it to flow through awareness without interference, remaining attuned to the naked awareness allowing its passage.

10. When you find yourself once again seizing upon an arising, look again into the thought, feeling or sensation that arises, refreshing your *seeing* of its ephemeral nature. And ease into the seeing of non-seeing.

Lucidity

Awareness, difficult for anyone to realize, is subtle, hard to comprehend, and seen by no one. It cannot be reified, but is equally present everywhere as the expanse of naturally occurring well-being.
— *Longchenpa*

The challenge and opportunity that comes on the heels of seeing through the I-process is to more deeply rest in the lucid openness of a not-I process. As it happens, moments of genuine lucidity open more often than we may recognize, especially for children at play and adults at ease. These moments occur while relaxing during an idle evening, making love or otherwise finding ourself alert in an unstressed, receptive frame of mind. Finding ourself that is, in a frame of mind that simply is, uncompelled with framing or not framing anything. In moments free of grasping, when seeing is just seeing, hearing is just hearing, feeling is just feeling, and we are not superimposing a commentary on the flow, we are already free and authentically present. But unless we are on the lookout for *this*, we may not recognize simple well-being for what it is.

We may – as compulsive thinking restarts – consider the freedom and ease of being to be merely an exceptional state of mind rather than our basic nature. This means we have already slipped out of openness as such into self-referencing. Propelled out of naked awareness, this slippage into reification occurs whether or not we are a meditator. As is said in Dzogchen, non-meditators do not get enlightened because they do not meditate, and meditators do not get enlightened because they do meditate. Fixating on meditative experiences within a project of pursuing enlightenment obscures the natural lightness of being.

Having glimpsed the empty-openness of self, it is important to recognize the in-dwelling lucidity of this glimpsing. Although nondual seeing is the crucial turn from compulsive thinking to the natural resilience of panoramic awareness, it may not be as elusive as we imagine. Everyday opportunities abound in ordinary shocks that momentarily interrupt our self-talk. The Tibetan word for a short, sharp shock that interrupts self-world narrating is *hedewa*. These are disruptions caused by a loud noise, unexpected surprise, orgasm or sneeze, for example, which stop the mind for a moment; creating a lucent gap if we are predisposed to notice it. If it is a sound that interrupts a train of thought, its value in this case will not be found in figuring out what made the sound, but in attuning to the lucidity that dawns as our internal dialogue stops. If it is an orgasm that crashes our mind's operating system, rather than following the pleasurable release into unconsciousness, we can linger in the openness of the bliss, which offers an entrée to lucid awareness. And if it is sneeze, we can recognize the instant presence that bursts opens in this abrupt interruption.

A couple of years after the glimpse with Ruth, I was sitting a three-month vipassana retreat. Towards the end of that time, I came into such ease and accord with the flow of experience that another glimpse occurred. As before, the spontaneous joy, equanimity and clarity of uncontrived presence suffused me. Only this time the glimpse was not brief but extended over hours and into the following day. During a regularly scheduled interview with one of the meditation teachers, I shared this blissful happening, assuming the sharing would be met with a recognition similar to the one I had with Ruth. So I was surprised when the instructor registered alarm at what I disclosed, exhorting me to "watch it." Meaning I should be suspiciously mindful of the bliss and spacious awareness as a meditative trap. I tried to explain that there was nothing "to watch," since the watcher and the watched were of the same nature. But rather than clarifying things, this further disconcerted my teacher. It was then I surmised that either I was not communicating this ineffable experience well enough or that the teacher was not able to recognize the difference between a meditative experience one could get attached to and awareness as such, in which no experience was being reified that might lend itself to attachment. Although I felt dismayed by the lack of communion I anticipated we would share, I also realized I was in need of a teacher who was able to guide me in deepening contentless awareness.

Fortunately, it was only a matter of months before I met Chogyal Namkhai Norbu. This meeting was one of a few in my life confirming the adage, *the teacher will appear when the student is ready.*

Relaxing the habit of fixating on whatever arises marks the pivotal shift of perspective into realizing *I* am not aware, awareness is aware. As a construed object dissolves, the construing subject vanishes. As the subjective self vanishes, the objective world of Otherness simultaneously dematerializes. This vanishing point of the mind reveals that subject and object are neither two different things nor are they the same thing. Dualistic vision collapses into the paradox that being is not other than non-being, as non-existence is unceasingly in a process of coming into existence.

If we wish to strengthen our ability to access authentic presence, this also need not be so difficult. In addition to being directly introduced to the nature of the mind by a qualified teacher, it is possible to discover and rediscover the natural spaciousness of awareness through formless meditations, which include enhanced practices of calm abiding.

Exercise 11a

Calm abiding without support

This practice has two parts. It begins with shifting the usual support of meditation from a material object of mindfulness to the immateriality of space. Rather than holding on to the handrail of a meditation object, calm abiding is evoked without a support. Focusing on no-thing, a calm mind rests on a space-like threshold advantageous for relaxing its intentional focus and seeing its contentless nature. This can be done either outdoors under a wide sky or inside.

1. Having calmed your system through meditation focusing on breathing, sensations and feelings, continue to abide in choiceless awareness supported by whatever is the dominant object of mindfulness.
2. Then, if your eyes are closed, gently open them. If you are outside under a clear sky, and it is not midday with a bright sun that could damage your eyes, you can cast your gaze away from the sun, perhaps with sunglasses, into the vastness of space. If you are inside, cast your gaze in the space midway between you and a wall, altar or whatever happens to be in front of you.
3. Either way, focus sharply at an invisible point in space. This makes for a triangular focus, in that the two eyes converge on a single point. The

sharpness of your concentration should momentarily block all thought. Hold this one-pointed concentration briefly if you are already calm, or longer if your mind is busy, draining thoughts of their energy. Keenly fix on this no point so your thoughts are effectively stilled.

4. Then, relax the sharpness of that concentrated focus. If you are sky-gazing, let your vision expand, merging with the space you are beholding. If you are focusing on a midpoint in space indoors, relax your focal point such that your peripheral vision expands and awareness becomes panoramic, taking in everything in the room but focusing on nothing in particular.

5. Inside or out, let your awareness rest in spacious alertness, allowing appearances (including the breath, sensory objects, feelings and thoughts) to freely arise and pass within this open field. Being aware of what is happening but without fixating or ignoring anything, abide in unsupported calm.

6. Enjoy the spacious presence. You can leave the meditation here and dedicate the merit if you like. Or, you can proceed as follows.

Exercise 11b

Dissolving calm abiding

7. Having focused on a no point and then released that fixation into spacious presence, notice that although the separation between outer perceptions and an inner perceiver has dissolved, you are totally cognizant within this empty-openness. At this vanishing point of mind, *see* wakeful awareness as such and let this non-seeing be.

8. There is nothing more to do. Doing anything more would be too much, so don't mess with it! Simply rest, basking in panoramic awareness and letting the simple recognition of this open presence saturate and recalibrate your system.

9. At some point, perceptions and thoughts will arise and the mind will fixate on something and begin cogitating. If you notice this quickly, rather than returning to an object of mindfulness such as the breath, sharply refocus your attention on a no point.

10. When you are again keenly focused on nothing with thoughts stilled, relax your concentration as before, allowing thoughts and feelings to arise as they will – but rest in the spacious awareness that allows their arising. You may feel a slight dizziness or lightness doing this. If so, that's fine, if not, that's fine too, as Tsoknyi Rinpoche is fond of saying.

11. This practice can be done as long as you like, as a quick glimpse or you can linger longer depending on your energy and situation. It is important not to strain yourself, but to clearly see the formless yet vivid nature of unfabricated mind.

15

Letting be

> To let be – that is, to let beings be as the beings which they
> are – means to engage oneself with the open region and its
> openness into which every being comes to stand, bringing
> that openness, as it were, along with itself.
>
> *– Martin Heidegger*

A MOMENT OF NONDUALISTIC VISION DISPERSES THE SELF-WORLD construction project through which we orient and insulate ourself. In the vanishing of reference points, the scales momentarily fall from our eyes. Heidegger and Meister Eckhart both referred to this glimpsing as a *moment of vision (augenblick)*. And they both seemed to feel a momentary glimpse was as good as it got; that the most that could be expected of contemplative presence was to have occasional flashes of clear seeing. In this, they underestimated the potential integration available to better informed and more seasoned yogins. More realized contemplatives know it is possible not only to have fleeting glimpses of lucid presence, but to settle more surely into a timeless moment of vision. While these illustrious seers certainly had the capacity for opening to nondual presence, they apparently lacked the skillful means to abide longer in naked awareness; and by doing so, to more fully integrate the spectacular diversity of mindstates into their nondual luminous nature.

Depending on our readiness for seeing through ourself, we will respond to a moment of vision in various ways. If we are well prepared for tolerating untethered openness, we will simply let the vanishing be. In letting openness linger, it more thoroughly saturates and rewires our system, insofar as "neurons that fire together, wire together." If we are somewhat prepared, we may find ourself briefly enthralled with the bliss, clarity or profound calm that can arise in being momentarily unbound. If we are not particularly prepared, we might disregard the whole thing, considering it an aberration. if we are ill-prepared, then *yikes!* We are likely to freak out in the groundlessness of being unfettered. If this happens, the door of self-perception may slam shut as we scramble to find some self-ground to hold onto. But whatever our capacity: resting, glimpsing, disregarding or panicking when we are nakedly present, the practice of *letting be* is the same.

Double rainbow of purpose

> To see through the self is to be liberated by everything that
> happens.
> — *Dogen*

If we are not well-prepared for naked openness, although we see the truth of non-self, we may not fully trust it. There are various ways ontological mistrust plays out. Being ill-prepared and finding ourself without a ground can feel like we are falling into an abyss, and we will react by scrambling to ground ourself. This is a turbocharged version of what happens when we wake up disoriented, perhaps from a dream or in a strange room we know not where, and panic for a moment until we recall who and where we are. In being ill-prepared – not yet having matured our capacity – an unexpected opening is premature. Premature openings often evoke existential panic such as occurred to Maggie. This shock may well result in the bolstering of a self-protective, defensive posture, which is why I generally favor an "easy does it" approach to opening up.

If we are but slightly prepared, and a moment of vision is fleeting, the powerful sense of well-being that arises with it may strike us as a wonderful, other-worldly aberration. We are then likely to interpret the glimpse as an altered state rather than recognizing it as our natural state. This is the kind of experience – corresponding to our capacity/degree of preparation – that leads us to become a seeker, stalking rarified states.

If we are somewhat more prepared, a glimpse of clear seeing will leave an unquestionable impression as happened to me with Ruth. Such an impression stays tacitly with us even as its vividness dims. (I suspect Meister Eckhart and Heidegger had, more or less, this sort of preparation.) A moment of luminous vision fades into memory even as the seed of that memory continues to germinate in the rich soil composting in ground consciousness (*alayavijnana*). Pushing to break through repressive barriers, it will sprout more or less swiftly depending on how we tend it. If we effectively ignore it, the glimpse will fade to black, and we will be left unsure as to what a moment of nondual vision actually was, and is. This kind of doubt cannot be dissolved rationally. It is not a question of intellectually deciding the difference between the mind and its essential nature. To dissolve this doubt, it is necessary to see clearly again, and in abiding longer in lucid awareness, to let the mystery of authentic presence impress itself more deeply upon us. Even through we have seen through the self-illusion and glimpsed the wonderment of being, a glimpse or two or even two hundred is probably not enough to dissolve the compulsion for self-grounding.

Still, seeing through ourself is quite moving; and if we are at least somewhat prepared for it, the accompanying release gives us a boost of energy and confidence. But if we are not able to let this energizing be, it becomes a catch if we succumb to wanting to catch it. The pride that can swell in moments of lucid presence, especially if we have been diligently stalking it, can feel like a victory we are happy to win. But if we get drunk on the power, bliss, clarity or calm in trying to hold onto it, we will surely lose it. Again, there is no way around this pitfall (spiritual materialism, glitch #2) – we have to go through it. Likewise, having repeated glimpses of clear seeing occurring on a daily, or even hourly basis does not mean we have totally opened our wisdom eye and unleashed selfless compassion to its full potential.

Even the Buddha, following his initial night of awakening, continued to sit in meditative lucidity for some time, letting the mind's natural potency come to full flower. For him, as for us, letting be is the supreme key that allows the full force of repressed fixations and karmic propensities to return, and in returning to be released, and in being released, marvelously! to bring us into deeper accord with being's luminous intent. Letting constrictions and compulsions dissolve as clarity and compassion expand is a double rainbow of noble purpose.

Natural release

> Seek not enlightenment; only, cease to cherish illusions.
> *– Seng T'san, 3rd Ch'an Patriarch*

There is nothing that facilitates release as thoroughly as unstressed openness. Letting everything be as it is creates a gravitational field of non-resistance, in which – as the Buddha discovered under the Bo tree – poisonous arrows of repressed and deep-seated karmic holdings spontaneously blossom into a flowering of enlightened presence.

As Garab Dorje[20] taught, seeing the total perfection of existence is realized through the practice of *non-distracted non-meditation*. This points to meditation that is non-meditative in the sense that it is effortless, yet remains viscerally aware and non-distracted in the sense of not being carried away with whatever arises. It is a practical way of describing the living experience of true integration.

Finally, if we are well-prepared for a moment of clarity, but momentarily caught in a fixation, letting things be that muddy way without perpetuating,

---

20 The first human teacher of Dzogchen on this planet.

rejecting or trying to improve it, is the most direct way of allowing compulsive thinking to naturally calm down, tune in and see through itself. Being in the pain and confusion of samsara is no problem, because pain and confusion only ever arise within the space of awareness; and there is nothing about spacious awareness that is in any way lacking or in need of improvement.

> The innate state, fresh in all its nakedness, is one of natural settling. Without having to be engaged in, meditated on, or analyzed, it is vibrant, limpid, steadfast, and immediately apparent. — *Longchenpa*

Resting in awareness as such, lucid well-being increasingly pervades our system, as we become more at home in being empty-open and naturally high. High in the usual sense of feeling lighter, happier and prone to levity; at home, since wanting to be anywhere other than here dissolves when nothing is missing. In the place of wanting, an overflowing springbox of experiencing – good, bad and indifferent – flows unimpeded, free of grasping and aversion. Continuing in uncontrived presence gives birth to the recognition that there is nothing that needs to be liberated. Non-action is the linchpin recognition in nondual traditions the world over that is totally liberating.

The play of presence

> The Way is easy for those who have no preferences.
> — *Seng T'san, 3rd Ch'an Patriarch*

It is important to recognize that non-action, or non-reaction, the more precise meaning of non-action, is not inaction, which implies passive withdrawal. Inaction is but another form of action/reaction that occurs when we deliberately do nothing. We do nothing either because we are afraid of putting ourself at risk, as in "not getting involved" or passive aggressively withdrawing in giving someone "the cold shoulder." Inaction can also be unintentional, like when we are shocked and do not know what to do, finding ourself momentarily frozen. But either form of inaction can also transform into non-reaction if we open and respond more nakedly to what is.

Within the flux of experience, seeing there is nothing lacking that we need to improve and nothing that is too much for us to handle, we are able to respond without hesitation or compulsion. To the extent our responses remain open (to feedback) and free (from being identified with as *mine*), they cannot help but be expressions of the evolutionary imperative of existence, saturating us in healing-bliss, as Peter Fenner so tenderly puts it. In *this*, we more readily recognize that synchronicity (Jung), which is ordinarily extolled as a rare and exceptional coincidence, is actually happening all the time. There is synchrony in existence that is pervasively intelligent and inconceivably meaningful. Since there are no exceptions to this – everything already being in sync whether or not we like it or are inspired to change it – synchronicity no longer refers to a unique coincidence, but reveals itself to be the essential nature of time.

Echoing the verses of Dogen, except emphasizing the play of presence rather than liberation from fixations, Jerry Garcia points to the value of "getting high" in tapping into the evolutionary thrust toward well-being. "To get really high is to forget yourself. To forget yourself is to see everything else. To see everything else is to become an understanding molecule in evolution, a conscious tool of the universe." (2021, p.27) Whether in improvisational music, art or conversation, being open and temporarily above – free of – self-imposed densities, actuates the mind's creative play. Just like thoughts think and sensations sense, openness settled in itself playfully responds without adhesion to a static responder. By turns creative, destructive and conservative – like the Hindu gods Brahma, Shiva and Vishnu – spontaneous presence flows in ecstatic, if incomprehensible, meaningfulness.

Letting realization sneak up on you

Whatever comes, let it come. Whatever goes, let it go. Seek nothing beyond what is.   – *Drukpa Kagyu proclamation*

Whatever arises, nothing need be done about it as long as we rest in non-reifying awareness. Fascination may be fascinating, but awareness of fascination is not. Lust may be lustful, but awareness of lust is not. Anger may be angry, but awareness of anger also is not. As Thaddeus Golas puts it, "The awareness of confusion is not confused. The awareness of insanity is not insane." (1971, p.53) The key point bears repeating: identifying with that which arises rather than the awareness within which it arises is the crux of human folly.

Even if we know that energizing preferences of liking and disliking set samsara in motion, trying to force an end to wanting does not work, since it is but another deployment of wanting. But as we let desires and aversions be without resisting or energizing them, they lose their energy source and realization is able to sneak up on us. Without resisting inner conflicts, contradictions and mixed feelings by seizing upon one side while rejecting the other, we allow reactive formations to dissolve into their ambiguous, fluid nature.

Recognizing that thoughts and perceptions are rolling waves reminds us that we are never apart from the ocean of awareness. Such seeing loosens our enthusiasm for self-grounding: making a big deal out of any particular psychic waves that break over us. It is not we that find liberation, liberation finds us. But only if we let it. The price of ceasing to strive (nirvana) having things our own way opens us to the arising of dark moods and passing of bright ones, giving all experiences leave – love – to flow as they will.

Without self-referencing the flux of experience, thereby twisting it and dividing ourself from it, we might open to the same enlightenment the Buddha opened to. As difficult as it is to describe this, he offered his best attempt to the student Bahiya in a Sutta of the same name.

> In seeing, there is only the seen; in hearing, only the heard; in sensing, only the sensed, in the cognized, only the cognized...then, Bahiya, there is no you in connection with that. When there is no you in connection with that, there is no you there. When there is no you there, you are neither here nor there nor somewhere between the two. This, just this, is the end of confusion.

Since our bodymind is so used to be jacked-up on the stimulants of like and dislike, hope and fear, when striving pauses, the lack of propulsion can feel like we have stalled and are missing the excitement of life. But what we are missing is only the hit of habitual fixes: the adrenalized activity that makes us feel we are alive and going somewhere. Until our system is able to rest in innate well-being, peace that arises when striving ceases can feel boring. Here again, if we are unable to remain present within boredom, we are liable to re-amp our system. At this point, the most potent remedy for being bored or anxious is to not apply a remedy, but to relax into the groundlessness of boredom-anxiety and let our system get more used to being untethered.

Letting be allows divided consciousness to heal through more fully inhabiting the way in which we are divided, such that inner separations subside into the potentiality of their undivided nature. Depending on our capacity – at any given moment – for tolerating naked presence, natural release occurs through increasingly effortless modes of self-liberation.

Modes of self-liberation

When liberated by everything that happens,
Your mind and body, as well as the minds and bodies of others
    drop away.
No trace of liberation remains,
And this no trace continues endlessly.   *— Dogen*

In regard to non-action, it would seem that doing nothing must be the easiest thing to do. But since non-doing cannot be done, it proves impossible to do. The velocity of compulsive thinking and reacting is persistent in trying to ground itself, whether we meditate or not.

Still fractured by the shattering I underwent following the death of my sister, I went on a series of psychedelic journeys and glimpsed with awe the immensity of being. At twenty years old, I saw the universe as *worlds within worlds, wheels within wheels, turning to eternity; purposeless, except to be.*[21] The impact of this was so profound I wrote it down so as not to forget. I need not have bothered. The glimpse was compelling enough and I was in such a broken-open state, I never completely forgot it. Yet, because I was quite unprepared for it and calculative thinking continued to run my life, neither did I completely remember it.

In order to integrate nondual vision and potentiate the intelligence of authentic presence, my self-system, like yours, has to be able to tolerate being undone. Both the felt actuality of that early glimpse and the one I had with Ruth a few years later faded soon after they arose. But due to the meditative training I was engaged in by then, the glimpse with Ruth left a more indelible impression that could be more skillfully tended.

Seeing the ineffable nature of mind, even if briefly, has a number of benefits. Not the least of which, for me, was dispelling the doubt that my early experiences of nonduality were properties of the psychedelic drugs I took rather than my own nature. But dispelling this doubt is still far from being able to rest in wonderment in an on-going way. Forgetfulness has been the norm for me, as it seems to be for most of us. Nevertheless, the good news in living a contemplative life is that the intervals between forgetting and remembering the Way (things truly are) become gradually shorter as we in-

---

21 This, as John Negru observed, is a moment of vision into Indra's Net. Referenced in the Atharva Veda and amplified in Huayan Buddhism, this is an envisioning of the cosmos depicting each individual being as part of a web of inter-being. Each individual node in Indra's Net is inter-related and inter-dependent with all other nodes. I seem to exist on my own, yet belong to, and am somehow responsible for, all. And, since the net of being - to which I belong - extends infinitely, I participate – whether or not I recognize it – in inconceivable boundlessness.

crease our familiarity with authentic presence. In Dzogchen, there are three general modes in which we gain familiarity with the spontaneous release of self-liberation. All three involve meeting whatever arises without fixating on it. Through recognizing and then resting in unfabricated awareness, habit formations and subtle tendencies flicker and – without being reified – dissolve into their spacious nature, leaving no trace. Getting increasingly comfortable with being radically open is the heart practice of Dzogchen.

Liberation through bare attention

The final step in the Team Mindfulness process is dropping the inquiry altogether and simply resting in the openness and clarity of space. — *Tsoknyi Rinpoche*

Given how unpracticed we are resting in wonderment, even seasoned meditators spend much of the day, most days, absorbed in some kind of distraction and self-talk. As Norbu Rinpoche once remarked, a practitioner who is able to remain in instant presence for even one-third of a day is already a "great practitioner." By which I understood him to mean a highly realized being such as a Bodhisattva or Mahasiddha. Our distractibility is such that even though we are devoted to a path of non-reaction, we can't stop micro-managing our experience. This being the case, it is skillful to repeatedly refresh our seeing that openness as such is the (no-) place to be. In practices of natural release, refreshing the recognition of our empty-open nature means leaving our stream of consciousness alone.

The entry-level way this is accomplished in Dzogchen is *liberation through bare attention* (*cher-drol*). This involves three steps. The first step is noticing we are caught up in something. The second is turning attention around and looking into who is caught. Upon seeing there is no substantial there there, the third step in to let ourself be in the non-seeing. It is this third step that goes beyond the practice of mindfulness to resting in no-mind fullness.

Recognizing we are compulsively thinking or emotionally reacting, liberation through bare attention on the fly occurs in the midst of confusion as we look into the thinker-reactor. Slight effort is necessary to turn attention back on itself in order to see there is nothing to see. Recognizing this, liberation occurs immediately in that moment, like suddenly recognizing the face of a friend. It may take a moment for the naked recognition to clarify, like rising mist dissolving in space. As projections withdraw, fixations dispel themselves without having to call upon remedies like therapy, prayer, mindfulness, tonglen, visualization or mantra recitation, for instance. Liberation through bare attention is non-gradual, like when we turn a light on in a room and the entire room is immediately illuminated, even if it takes us a moment to adjust to the light. It is not necessary to focus on, attune to and release one fixation at a time, since all confusion is dispelled at once. In letting lucid awareness go on being, fixations that arise continue to lift spontaneously, like clouds dispersing in blue sky.

Exercise 12a

Look/see

As you watch your mind, you discover your self as the watcher. When you stand motionless, only watching, you discover yourself as the light behind the watcher. The source of light is dark, unknown is the source of knowledge. That source alone is. Go back to that source and abide there.
— *Nisargadatta Maharaji*

Liberation through bare attention works by looking within and seeing through who is doing the looking. This reversal of attention is not restricted to a meditation cushion, can be practiced anywhere at any time. While it is common to a number of Buddhist, Advaita Vedanta and other nondual traditions, I first came across this mode in a book on Ch'an (Zen) Buddhism (Lu K'uan Yu, 1970) prior to meeting Norbu Rinpoche. It is presented there as a practice of looking into the head of a thought. I received similar practices from a handful of teachers, but the one I am sharing here comes from Urgyen Tulku Rinpoche through Tsoknyi Rinpoche. I have found this version easy to understand and apply. It involves attending to the four movements of *looking out, looking in, seeing* and *resting* in spacious awareness. Looking out in order to rivet attention and be here now; looking in to see who is looking; seeing that the seer is no one and no thing apart from the seeing; and resting in this empty-openness.

There are two common sticking points in this practice that echo the two glitches mentioned earlier. The first arises at the point of looking within, when clarity is blocked at the start. The second occurs upon seeing clearly, when resting in openness degrades into fixation. The exercise proceeds as follows.

1. *Look out* at whatever is happening, including if it is an inner sensation. Simply notice what is with bare attention, without elaboration.

2. Then *look within* to see who is looking.

3. *See* there is no seer, only seeing.

4. If the recognition of lucid presence is not obvious, you have hit the first snag. In this case, do not press yourself, but look again, inquiring: *Do I as the looker have a shape, color or location? Am I on the inside or outside?* If you seem to have a shape or location, then consider, *Where is the boundary separating "me" and "not me"?* It is important to go carefully with this. This inquiry can be done either alone or with a partner.

5. If you still think you have found a seer who is other than the seen and the seeing, further inquiry is necessary.[22] Proceed to ask, *Who knows this knowledge?* or *Who is thinking this thought?* If you, or your partner in a dyad, come up with some version of "'I' am thinking this," then look into that: Who is thinking "'I' am thinking this?" And if you or your partner answer, "'I' am thinking that 'I' am thinking this," then look into that: *Who is thinking* "'I' am thinking that 'I' am thinking this?' And if the answer to that is not outright laughter but some version of "'I' am thinking that 'I' am thinking that 'I' am thinking this," then continue to look into, *Who is thinking* that "'I' am thinking that 'I' am thinking that 'I' am thinking this?"

6. By this point, the circular logic of conceptual thinking usually exhausts itself, collapsing into absurdity as a joyful sense of awe dawns in seeing there is nothing to see and that this seeing is boundless and benevolent.

7. If the mind clenches, and is insistent in positing a self-ground, let the whole exercise go. And without so much as a wisp of self-blame, emphasize foundational practices such as exercises #3 – 11 that work better for you.

8. If the mind can tolerate its undoing, then simply relax in naked presence.

It is at this point, in resting, that the second sticking point occurs. After awhile, lingering in lucid awareness may lose its crispness of clarity, slipping into a drowsy, dreamy state. Resting peacefully, we might not notice that the vividness of naked awareness has degraded into ground consciousness. The tip-off that holistic awareness has decayed into divided consciousness is the formation of a sense that I am having an experience. With this slight separation, *wanting* reasserts itself and we find ourself preferring the ease of being to unease. Wham! We are back in dualistic vision.

Yet again, there is no way around this bypass, since as our defenses collapse, awareness naturally opens to more subtle fixations and latent imprints. And since we have a strong inclination to want to be contented and at peace, we prefer to remain in the calm waters of a quasi-nirvana. Slipping from the liveliness of naked awareness into the ground of consciousness, we can linger

---

22 The thoroughness of this looking, as well as the fine-grained inquiry of Exercises #1 and #10, is informed by Peter Fenner's work. (2015, p.160&161)

contentedly in non-reactivity. At this depth, like the deeps of an ocean, consciousness is a neutral state having no currents or waves. The happy news is that since there is not a streaming of consciousness, no further karma can be created. Less happy is that latent karmic tendencies/repressions remain temporarily blocked and cannot be released.

Nevertheless, being settled in deep calm is helpful in two big ways. First, this lets our system become more familiar with being non-reactive and at peace. Habituating to deeper settledness – that famous Buddhistic calm – is like depositing money in a bank. It provides an accumulation (of merit) we can later draw upon to more ably pacify fixations when they arise. Not only to more ably pacify fixations when they arise, but to more completely liberate them. Secondly, given the persistence of enlightened intent, being in a state of deep calm – if not grasped onto – eventually surfaces the seeds of primal repression, affording the opportunity to release our core fixation. Allowing resting in spacious awareness to morph into releasing, we find release happens naturally as long as untethered resting continues.

Exercise 12b

Look/see-rest/release

9. When a thought, feeling or sensation arises that carries us away, look again into that movement of mind. See there is nothing there, like a cloud dissipating.
10. Rest in the seeing.
11. Notice that experience is sometimes calm and settled, sometimes in motion, Arising in so many ways: groggy or dull, sharp or clear, with emotional texture happy or sad, angry or blissful, in infinite flux.
12. See that whatever arises is of the same wakeful nature.
13. On the basis of perceptions, concepts will form to identify, elaborate or explain what is happening. See that this narration is just another arising and let it be.
14. As what arises naturally releases back into The Mystery, continue resting in presence as such.
15. This is another practice that at first is best to do in short periods. Practice sessions will organically lengthen as your system becomes more in sync with being's unimpeded, unceasing spontaneity. As we become more familiar with non-distracted, lucid presence, it morphs into increasingly effortless modes of self-liberation.

Liberation upon arising

All experience, inner and outer,
is like a dream, an illusion, a bubble, and a shadow,
like dew and lightning.
Thus should you contemplate it.   — *Diamond Sutra*

When we are able to abide a little more surely in unfabricating presence, letting experience be in both its movement and rest, perceptions and concepts liberate themselves *upon arising (shar-drol)*. This is a mode of near-effortless release, in which fixating tendencies dissolve as (rather than after) they arise, like drawing on water. Here, exerting anything but the slightest effort is unnecessary, and actually an obstruction. Awareness at this point is sufficiently settled-in-unsettledness and panoramically open to the point where we are able to abide for awhile in lucid equipoise. Thoughts, feelings and sensations auto-release as they come up. In the mindstream's unimpeded flow, percepts and concepts form like clouds amassing, and without being interfered with, naturally disperse into their radiant nature. In this, there is no need to intentionally look out and in. Reaction formations self-dissolve into the lightness of being. As Norbu Rinpoche puts it,

> Even passions that would condition someone who has not reached this level of practice can simply be left as they are. This is why it is said that all one's passions, all one's karmic vision, become just like ornaments in Dzogchen, because without being attached to them, one simply enjoys them as the play of one's own energy, which is what they are. (1986, p.118)

In this Way, the energy bound in tensions both gross and subtle spontaneously release, potentiating compassionate responses within an expanse of intimate wonderment.

Even so, in this advanced mode of natural release, when we have the capacity to let things be as they are, unfold as they will and rest in healing-bliss, a habituation to clinging is likely to persist. A witness consciousness may still be subtly tracking what is happening. With this ever so slight referencing, it can be tempting to both develop a quiet satisfaction with our victory and grasp onto sublime states. When this glitch happens, it is like grasping the thorny stem of a blooming rose. We lose touch with the flowering of *being* in attending to the pain of a pricked finger. But this slight distraction need not be a problem as long as we recognize our grasping and – depending on our capacity – either downshift into bare attention by *looking/seeing-resting/release* once again, or, in that very recognition allow our grasping to self-release. How could there be anything more beneficial than this?

Well, it might be even better not to prick our fingers at all. It might be better to liberate grasping at its inception as the impulse potentiates, before its actual arising. Instantaneous, unexcelled self-liberation becomes possible as we more deeply trust it as a reflex beyond our will, surrendering ourself more fully to the impulse of enlightened intent. Opening to this potentiality confirms we are able to rest in naked awareness covered only by the most delicate of veils. This is the cognizance that knows our innermost veil cannot be lifted by anything we do or do not do. It can only lift itself.

Unexcelled self-liberation

If no attempt is made to contrive suchness, then like the sky unobscured by clouds, there is ever-lucid timeless radiance.
– *Longchenpa*

In contrast to the Sutra path renouncing negativities, grasping and self-importance, and the Tantra path transforming emotional reactions into non-reactivity, is the pathless path of Self-Liberation proper. Natural release here occurs 100% effortlessly. Recognizing that experience *as it is* is already of the nature of spontaneous presence, and the experiencer of nowness is not other than awareness as such, spiritual paths collapse as we become fully participatory in *being's* endless, ecstatic play.

All three modes of natural release are generally referred to as self-liberation, since none appeal to psychological insight, behavioral modification, spiritual progress, moral correction, meditative practice or any yogic technique other than being wholly present *just now*. Each mode relies solely on the wakefulness innate to awareness in letting things and beings be as they are. But spontaneous liberation awakened through the contemplative yogas of *bare attention* and *upon arising* still involve a slight effort in tuning attention to itself. Thus they are preliminary, if in a quite advanced way, to wholly effortless, *unexcelled self-liberation* (*rang-drol*) proper. In this, whatever begins to arise self-releases instantaneously like a snowflake touching water or a snake uncoiling itself, without the intervention of witness consciousness. It is only at this point that Norbu Rinpoche said one can consider oneself a true dzogchen practitioner.

Once we gain some familiarity with letting things be, and our system is re-calibrating itself to tolerate untethered presence, it can happen that ordinary experiences, especially passionate ones, may jolt us into spontaneous release. One moment we are caught up in an emotional reaction, the next, *Bang!* we see the folly of the thing and find ourself suddenly free, perhaps laughing out loud at human folly.

Opening unconditionally and resting in openness, without grasping for any reference point or seeking any further liberation, it is possible to come into such perfect accord with the pulse of being that remnant kinks in our deep unconscious uncoil. Enlightened intent is given free reign to move, evolve and settle as it will. The practice at this point is the non-practice of continuing to relax in unconditional openness.

> By resting in naturally occurring timeless awareness, one experiences the yoga of suchness.   — *Longchenpa*

As our system settles more confidently into wakeful awareness, evolution proceeds apace such that self-liberation occurs even more effortlessly than a snake uncoiling itself. The natural release here is likened to a thief entering an empty house. Any distinction between an arising and a dissolving vanishes in an immediacy in which all cogitation passes into contemplation. Like a thief who enters a house expecting to find something finds there is nothing to find, this pinnacle play of presence occurs beyond a sense of liberation or captivity. Even the most subtle karmic seed-anticipation does not germinate, being already fully integrated in spacious awareness. There is nothing to find, nothing to steal, nothing to return to its natural state. This is what is meant when it is said enlightenment provides neither harm nor benefit. In unfabricated suchness, there is nothing to gain and nothing to lose, everything being complete and perfect as it is.

> I have not gained the least thing from supreme enlightenment, and that is called supreme enlightenment.
>   — *The Diamond Sutra*

Beware the Balrog

> Since there is no attainment, awakened beings abide by means of transcendent knowledge. And since there is no obscurity of mind, they have no fear, transcend falsity and pass beyond the bounds of sorrow.   — *The Heart Sutra*

As letting be suffuses our mind and repressive barriers lift, the multitudes within, as Walt Whitman put it, emerge. So, even as we settle more confidently into untethered freedom and ease of being, it is prudent to also beware. Deeper unfolding may be disruptive for you and those around you. For instance, you may find yourself less accommodating if being nice has been integral to your coping style; or more sexually engaging if eroticism has been something you have avoided, or more chaste; or less social if contemplative solitude is what you have been delaying, or more social; or more generous in a random and perhaps conventionally irresponsible way if you have coped with insecurity by being a bit tight; or, you name it. Because they tend to be overshadowed in spiritual texts by the bright flowerings of peace, bliss and clarity, I feel darker upwellings that come out through de-repression deserve due attention. Even when we have high capacity and are well along on the path, these arisings are to be expected, as with the Buddha under the Bo.

There is a poignant scene in J.R.R. Tolkien's epic fantasy, *Lord of the Rings: The Fellowship of the Ring*, in which the mighty wizard, Gandalf, having just maneuvered a miraculous escape for the fellowship he is guiding through a cavernous, haunted mountain labyrinth, trails them across a tenuous fairy bridge to freedom. They had just fought and evaded a horde of Orcs and Goblins – symbolic of our worst, ugliest tendencies – when a still more menacing primeval force brooding in the mountain's dour depths emerges to hinder their passage: a Balrog. Frightened but undeterred, Gandalf stands to face this demonic force. Staff in hand (one-pointed, undistracted), he battles the inchoate mass, smiting him with a blow that casts the beast back into the abyss from whence it came. With a swell of relief, he turns triumphant to his worried band. But just as he turns, the slenderest wisp of demonic fire reaches out of the chasm to snare him round the ankle, dragging him into nether regions he thought he had escaped. Even though an accomplished wizard like Gandalf may have mastered all manner of dark impulses, dispelling fear and confusion by seeing through coarse and subtle fixations, this does not mean he is totally victorious. There remains the matter of still more subtle compulsions and imprints. Not to mention the innermost repression that generates the wanting for self-grounding to begin with.

As repressions lift, released energy boosts the power of self-mastery and heightens sensitivity. If we let these be such that an increase in personal power is balanced by relational sensitivity, and vice versa, all goes quite well. But if our enhanced power and sense of vulnerability should diverge, by identifying with either one or the other, we could be in for a Balrog-like trial. Through fixating on either side, raw power or raw vulnerability bounce back on us, re-energizing divided consciousness and blocking a more complete liberation. If this happens, as McLeod notes,

> …two things happen. The higher level of energy in your system flows into the reactive pattern, making it stronger. The higher energy also flows into the repressing pattern, making that stronger. Both the reactive patterns of the emotion and their repression are reinforced. You end up splitting in two. One part of you is capable of [enhanced] attention and response. The other part becomes increasingly rigid and inflexible. (2001, p.88)

When released energy bounces back into reactive formations and vulnerability is repressed, compassion is impaired. This can inflate a monstrous sense of self possessed by power. Instead of letting being(s) be and giving ourself to unconditional presence, we identify with the high energy, inflating ego. If this happens, since we have enough awareness to sense that an inner split is happening, we are likely to fall into a (*Vajra*) hell of acute inner conflict. This is especially a danger for persons with charismatic and/or controlling proclivities of self-grounding. It is from a power position that various kinds of abuse and misconduct are perpetrated.

Deepening presence may also potentiate forms of clarity such as clairvoyance and clairaudience. As mentioned earlier, it is possible to mistake these extraordinary states of mind for the innate nature of mind. Displays of clarity as well as sublime states of bliss and non-thought are side effects – ornaments – of authentic presence. If these natural arisings are not seized upon and allowed to flow without interference, they cannot help but flower as compassionate expressions. But if we become captivated by them, thinking ourself awakened or superior to others, they function as entrapments; both for the person so identifying and whoever falls under their influence. This is particularly a danger on paths that cultivate altered states, high energy and psychic powers as prime goals.

Because high energy states are so juicy, it can seem – to the extent we have not integrated them – that in regard to their pizzazz, simply being pales in comparison. But extraordinary mindstates inevitably morph and pass. And when that happens, a fixating tendency we have been ignoring will return, like a Balrog from the depths. But when states of psychic power remain permeated by sensitivity, the vulnerability of wakeful awareness polices itself.

On the other hand, should we identify with the vulnerability that comes with undefended openness, we run the risk of impairing the discriminating power that cuts through passivity and empatheosis. Being possessed by vulnerability is especially a danger for sensitive persons prone to grounding themselves by accommodating to others, being nice, a good guy or a compulsive peacemaker in order to avoid conflict. Becoming captivated in a vulnerable, empathic, compulsively helpful position ironically leads to helplessness. This sort of identification inclines us toward being dominated by others, situations or our own depressive ("I should be doing more and better") thoughtforms.

Whether the energy boost that comes with natural release gets appropriated into a dominating position of power or a submissive position of vulnerability, liberation is blocked. While these coarse sorts of fixation may awaken something like a Balrog, more subtle and less troublesome holdings can arise that hinder a more thorough liberation. Prominent among these is the compulsion to hold onto meditative methods and religious rituals when we no longer need to do so.

Beyond method

> In reality there is no formula which gives rise to the highest,
> must fulfilled awakening.   *– Diamond Sutra*

At the point of resting in a seeing that is without a seer or something to be seen, meditation practices that seek to accomplish something become obstacles. As Tsoknyi Rinpoche observes, "this is something we can understand only in our experience, if we train. Otherwise we can listen to thousands of hours of talk about this, and it'll never get clear." (1998, p.94) To the extent we are able to let the lightness of being be, we have already arrived at the further shore of genuine freedom. Our diligence in training has paid off. The preparatory vehicle we have been traveling in has enabled us to reach our goal. Abiding in effortless presence, any further effort to improve what is by trying to stay open, maintain a calm state, deepen or prolong blissful presence, or see more clearly than we already do, can and should be relinquished.

Without any separate thing to meditate on, and without getting carried away in distraction, it is at this point that clinging to a habitual method of meditation gets in the way. Delighting in the lightness of being, we want this freedom and ease to continue. And due to this ever so delicate wanting, we put an ever so delicate finger on the scale of our experiencing, subtly manipulating its flow to perpetuate a luminous state. This always fails. To the extent we try to improve The Flow, we wind up obstructing the spontaneity of bliss, clarity and ecstatic openness from continuing to emerge...dissolve... and re-emerge as the free and lively play it is.

> Whatever happens let it happen; whatever manifests, let it shine,
> Whatever arises let it dawn and whatever occurs just let it be;
> And, moreover, whatever is anything let it be nothing at all.
>   *– Longchenpa*

Rather than freeing us, meditation practices bind us whenever we try to improve being as such. In the wakeful expanse of instant presence, seeking to correct anything at all reflects a remnant effort to be in control and buffer the awe-fullness of authentic presence. What makes awe in the face of The Mystery awful, is a lack of trust in being. When this happens, it is helpful to again look into our doubt, recognize it as self-referencing, see it has no basis, and proceed to let it release like a snake uncoiling itself.

Even though I weaned myself from a meditation timer once I became a Dzogchen practitioner, I still found it difficult to not measure my spiritual progress, especially during personal retreat. Early on – by which I mean a period not less than thirty years! – I would establish a daily personal retreat schedule of meditation sessions lasting a pre-determined length of time. For someone new to solitary retreat, making a schedule is certainly a good idea to corral a distractible mind. But eventually, the imposition of periods of enforced meditation become superfluous, or even a kind of self-torture, as happened to me for a time. It took consistent self-coaching over years to break myself of this compulsion and yield more nakedly to the ebb and flow of *now*. Competing with myself by measuring minutes, hours, days or weeks spent on a cushion, I fed the illusion that liberation was something that I was able, or at least should be able, to accomplish.

Beyond wanting

Gate, gate, paragate, parasamgate, bodhi svaha!
– *Heart Sutra*

This verse, meaning *Gone, gone, gone beyond, gone beyond the very notion of beyond, wakefulness as such!* celebrates the victory of a liberation that is no longer constrained by ambition. In seeing through constructs and letting The Flow be, we rest in openness free of the projections of divided consciousness, including notions of undivided consciousness. Beyond being captivated as a theyself, this goneness is beyond the temptation to want anything other than what is happening. Being beyond fixation is a negative way of announcing what authentic presence is free from. Being free from self-centredness can likewise be celebrated in a positive sense, that within the flow of self-existing awareness, we are released into the fullness of (human) being. Resting in un-stressed equipoise, there is nothing beyond *this* we are lacking and nothing that needs improvement. We have gone beyond wanting.

With nothing excluded to an outside or included on an inside, un-bound openness and unhesitating responsiveness discloses itself as the lived actuality of dzogchen: total completion, natural perfection, complete fulfillment. In a formal sense, Dzogchen is translated in these words as the title of a Tibetan tradition describing a nondualistic view, contemplative yogic practices, and integration of that view and practice in daily life. But in its informal, essential sense, dzogchen is another word for basic freedom, the totally fulfilling, natural perfection of existence as it is.

Just as we cannot say how unconditional love and spontaneous clarity will express themselves until they do, we cannot know how deeply held fixations will release until they do. In my case, for sudden, if brief, liberation to occur when it did during my marital quarrel, I must have readied myself more than I knew. The ecstatic collapse of my self-position took me completely by surprise, even though Norbu Rinpoche suggested over and over again this could happen.

My not knowing the depth of my own capacity is not unusual. I have since observed many times over how therapy clients, Dharma students, Vajra siblings, family members and friends often misjudge themselves. Sometimes, we narcissistically think we have more capacity than we do and succumb to spiritual bypassing. Other times, and once again I feel this is the greater and more common misjudgment, we underestimate ourselves. Habituated to wanting, we are driven by a sense of inadequacy, so it makes sense to not completely trust our (calculating) mind. To the extent we hang on to a self-ground, we do not see that the nature of that mind is completely trustworthy. The truth is, we are less precious than we think we are and more precious than we realize.

I believe we each sense our true nature more than we are prepared to admit, for the simple reason that making this admission means unmaking *me*. It is for this reason that having a heart relationship with a qualified master, teacher or spiritual friend who is more at ease in naked presence than us is of inestimable value.

Relational gravity and the transmission of presence

There is no "buddhahood," only suchness.
— *Longchenpa*

While dark, Balrog-like forces can pull us down, being in relationship to a being of lightness can give us a lift – contact high – in the direction of unconditioned wakefulness. There are various pointing-out instructions and relational exchanges in nondual traditions through which a teacher directs a student's attention to innate awareness. The classic Zen analogy of a master pointing a finger toward the moon captures the gist of this communication. It depicts that the point of the teaching is not the pointing finger but the moon being pointed to. This analogy is invoked as a corrective to dispel the confusion of a student who thinks it is the teacher, technique or the teachings that are the point of practice, rather than wakefulness as such. Without taking this understanding to heart, the Buddha, Dharma and Sangha remain a fetish, as we miss the point of the whole thing.

Pointing-out usually occurs conceptually (as in these pages) as we consider what authentic presence is, such that conceptual thinking opens itself, touching into The Mystery. In the Tibetan tradition, pointing-out is also referred to as transmission, empowerment (*wangkur*) or initiation (*abhisheka*), which, in addition to conceptual introduction, can be conveyed either symbolically or intuitively/mind to mind.

A non-conceptual, symbolic communication occurs when a master uses a symbolic form, such as a mirror, *vajra*, crystal, or gesture, to convey uncontrived presence. Brisk Zen confrontations, like a master hitting a student with a slipper when they are on the verge of *seeing*, are of this order. The critical factor with symbolic pointing-out is there must be readiness on the part of the student, and a teacher attuned to a student's readiness (or potential readiness) in order for nonverbal communication to get across. There are also elaborate Tibetan ceremonies of initiation, involving an invocation, a blessing with sanctified water, the repetition of mantras and arcane ritual procedures. These extravagant performances have an advantage for some people, insofar as a person devoted to and confident in Tibetan Buddhism is motivated to pay keen attention during a special empowerment, waiting for "it" to happen. But the exotic nature of these rituals may also make for a fascination that distracts from the invisible mystery being shared. The sharing of lucid presence certainly does not depend on any formal ceremony and can just as effectively, or more effectively, be presented in very simple, informal exchanges if student and teacher are ready for it.

Mind to mind transmission is the epitome of informal, direct sharing. This involves a relational exchange in which the ineffable but lucid presence of awareness is shared instantaneously, unmediated by concepts or symbols. As a direct introduction, mind to mind transmission entails the mutual recognition that wakeful, self-liberating awareness is beyond all effort, right here, just now. Even though no thing is either transmitted or received, the relational vividness of this sharing confirms nothing could possibly be left out.

16

It all comes down to this

To waste one's precious human rebirth on trivial concerns is a tragedy. Only practice leads to one's own realization, and only through one's own realization can one ultimately help others, manifesting the capacities to be able to guide them to attain that same state themselves; any material assistance one can offer can only ever be provisional. To be able to help others one must therefore begin by helping oneself, however contradictory that may sound.   *– Chogyal Namkhai Norbu*

TO BECOME FULLY HUMAN, FULL LIBERATION MUST BE OUR OVERRIDING LIFE goal. Even as the evolutionary achievement of humanity arises through a primal repression of our essential wholeness, (this dividing of) consciousness presents us with an unparalleled opportunity. Driven by primal wanting for the wholeness we have lost, the disquiet, if not estrangement of the human condition is a reliable goad of innate intelligence. The niggling of our discontent, amplified by trying to escape this predicament, motivates the creation of a self-ground, reifying into *a story of me*. Yet it is this story, and the anxious discontent it augurs, that provides motivation for befriending the pain and waking up to how we are out of sync with what is. As we tune in more deeply to the way things actually are, our inner separation folds in on itself, surfacing the gross and subtle fixations that perpetuate our sense of apartness.

Depending on your capacity and life situation, you may find it best to proceed slowly and gradually. Calming down, tuning in and better understanding the story of who you and others have been telling about you. Befriending the felt embodiment of that illusion, it becomes increasingly possible to see through it and let yourself more nakedly be the being/*being* you are. Or, if you wish and are able, you can proceed directly to the instantaneous presence of well-*being*, opening yourself just now! to the ecstatic freedom of what always already is.

> Abandon yourself in imperturbable rest, for this is the very
> consummation of enlightened intent.   – *Longchenpa*

Either way, in opening to nowness we cannot help but become permeable to a summons from enlightened intent. Even though karmic reactivity ceases in moments of authentic presence, the river of time does not stop flowing. Beings caught in its currents continue to circle endlessly. Without a barrier between yourself and others, you cannot help but feel their plight and respond compassionately to their pain, as it were your own. Of course, within nondual lucidity, the wonderment of existence including the plight of the beings in it, is not reified or made into some joyless, compulsive mission. Since there is no attachment to an outcome apart from open-ended, dream-like relationship as such, success and failure become meaningless. Being essentially free – untethered – you can help others as you are so inclined and capable as circumstances permit. You can also simply and innocently retire to solitary or shared contemplation, delighting in being, swimming in the currents and eddies of mystery.

To conclude, words of peerless Longchenpa (14th C.) far surpass anything I might say.

> When I think about the present evil times, I feel intensely
> discouraged.
> Our lives provide us with no real leisure, for we waste them on the
> path of distraction.
> There is no possibility of fathoming all that is to be known, and no
> end to conceptual elaboration.
> Therefore, day and night, pursue spiritual practice that focuses on
> the heart essence of being.
> You will die before completing all you wish to do in this life;
> One thing leads to another, like the waves of the ocean.
> Come to thoroughly appreciate that nothing you undertake will be
> useful when you die.
> From today on, practice to attain enlightenment, which brings
> liberation.
> Where will you end up? What will happen? What can you know?
> Who can help you?
> How can you develop the confidence to be content and fearless in
> this life?
> Therefore, while you have some self-determination,
> It is time to strive for the lasting state of liberation.
> Remember that your body, wealth, family, friends, and experiences
> in this life will all be left behind as you go forth alone with no

one to accompany you.

It is time to seek a refuge and protector to be with you then.

Things will not always remain as they are now;

When the Lord of Death comes for you, throwing heaven and earth into turmoil, what will you do?

At that moment, in whom or what will you place your hopes?

Therefore, put the sacred dharma into practice now.

Whether or not you rely on the wise and powerful, whether or not you yourself are learned, the hour of your death approaches; rouse the forces of virtue.

Meditate on what is genuinely meaningful – mind itself, the heart essence of being.

Then the happiness and joy of higher realms will be ensured.

You will be welcomed by victorious ones to the precious palace of noble liberation.

You will experience the ultimate state of supreme bliss, forever unchanging,

And the absolutely infinite wealth of enlightenment, sublime, self-knowing timeless awareness.

I, a beggar lacking any spiritual qualities, exhort you with these words.

This is my heart advice for your benefit; keep it in mind![23]

---

23 Translation by Richard Barron, 2006, p.252&253.

Further resources

Calming Down

Johnson, W. (2012). *Breathing through the whole body*. Rochester, VT: Inner Traditions.

Kabat-Zinn, J. (2013) *Full catastrophe living: Using the wisdom of your body and Mind to face stress, pain, and illness*. (Revised edition). NY: Random House.

Miller, R. C. (2015). *The iRest program for healing PTSD*. Berkeley, CA: New Harbinger.

Mipham, L. (1973). *Calm and clear*. (K. Dowman, Trans.) Berkeley, CA: Dharma.

Tuning In

Bugental, J. (1999). *Psychotherapy isn't what you think: Bringing the therapeutic engagement into the living moment*. Phoenix, AZ: Zeig-Tucker.

Gendlin, E. T. (1978). *Focusing*. New York, NY: Bantam.

Goldstein, J. (1983). *The experience of insight*. Boulder, CO: Shambhala.

Heidegger, M. (1966). *Discourse on thinking*. (Trans. J. Anderson and E. H. Freund). NY: Harper Colophon. (Original work published 1959)

Prendergast, J. J. (2015). *In touch: How to tune in to the inner guidance of your body and trust yourself*. Boulder, CO: Sounds True.

Wegela, K. K. (2009). *The courage to be present*. Boston, MA: Shambhala.

Deepening

Brach, T. (2003). *Radical acceptance: Embracing your life with the heart of a Buddha*. New York, NY: Bantam.

Chodron, P. (1994). *Start from where you are*. Boston: Shambhala.

Chodron, P. (1997). *When things fall apart: Heart advice for difficult times*. Boston: Shambhala.

Epstein, M. (1998). *Going to pieces without falling apart: A Buddhist perspective on wholeness*. NY: Broadway.

Foster, J. (2016). *The way of rest: Finding the courage to hold everything in love*. Boulder, CO: Sounds True.

Levine, P. (1997). *Waking the tiger: Healing trauma*. Berkeley, CA: North Atlantic.

Prendergast, J.J. (2019). *The deep heart: Our portal to presence*. Boulder, CO: Sounds True.

Seeing

Fenner, P. (2007). *Radiant mind: Awakening unconditioned awareness*. Boulder, CO: Sounds True.

Hixon, L. (1993). *Mother of all Buddhas: Meditation on the Prajnaparamita Sutra*. Wheaton, IL: Quest Books.

Kelly, L. (2015). *Shift into freedom: The science and practice of open-hearted awareness*. Boulder, CO: Sounds True.

Surya Das. (1997). *Awakening the Buddha within*. New York, NY: Broadway.

Trungpa, C. (1976). *The myth of freedom*. Boston, MA: Shambhala.

Tsoknyi, R. (2012). *Open heart, open mind: Awakening the power of essence love*. NY: Harmony Books.

Letting Be

Namkhai Norbu. (1986). *The crystal and the way of light: Sutra, tantra and dzogchen*. (J. Shane, Ed.). NY: Routledge.

Trungpa, C. (1981). *Journey without goal: The Tantric wisdom of the Buddha*. Boulder, CO: Shambhala.

Tsoknyi, R. (1998). *Carefree dignity: Discourses on training in the nature of mind*. Boudhanath, Nepal: Rangjung Yeshe.

Selected Dzogchen source texts

Dowman, K. (Trans.). (2010). *Natural perfection: Longchenpa's radical dzogchen*. Boston, MA: Wisdom.

Dowman, K. (Trans.). (1994). *The flight of the garuda: Teachings of the Dzokchen tradition of Tibetan Buddhism*. Boston, MA: Wisdom.

Longchen(pa) Rabjam. (2001). *A Treasure Trove of Scriptural Transmission: A Commentary on the Precious Treasure Basic Space of Phenomena*. (R. Barron, Trans.) Junction City, CA: Padma.

Longchenpa. (1976). *Kindly bent to ease us, part 3: Wonderment*. (H.V. Guenther, Trans.) Emeryville, CA: Dharma.

Longchenpa. (1987). *You are the eyes of the world*. (K. Lipman & M. Petersen, Trans.) Novato, CA: Lotsawa.

Low, J. (Trans.). (1994). *Simply being: Texts in the Dzogchen tradition*. London: Vajra.

List of Exercises

Acknowledgements

THIS, LIKE ALL BOOKS, IS SITUATED WITHIN A CONVERSATION BENEFITTING from the contributions of many people. The psychological ideas and yogic pointers herein have taken shape by virtue of countless exchanges with heart teachers, Dharma friends, therapy colleagues and academic collaborators over many years. Equally important are the psychotherapy clients, Dharma students, assorted truth seekers and graduate psychology students – many now esteemed colleagues and spiritual friends – who participated in the courses, formal trainings, retreats, and informal groups I have offered. Together with the wisdom and compassion of my teachers, it is the confusion, misery, fervent questions and raw candor of clients, students and friends that deserve special mention. Their honest distress and heartfelt dilemmas along with my own, motivated me to clarify things for all of us. It is my good fortune that there are far too many of these valuable interlocutors to acknowledge by name.

Even so, in addition to my Dharma and Dzogchen teachers mentioned throughout, I wish to express particular gratitude to John Prendergast and Peter Fenner, who have steadfastly encouraged me during the long arc of the writing to keep going. Since they are both exemplars at integrating psychological and spiritual knowledge with therapeutic presence and nondual wisdom, I found their enthusiasm and confidence in my work to be reassuring when my own doubts arose. Lama Surya Das encouraged me early on to be bold in presenting Dzogchen in experience-keyed, psychological language. And Bonnie Landfield, Mary Smyer and Amy Conway in particular touched me with their sincerity in asking me to keep teaching and writing. More generally, the John F. Kennedy University School for Holistic Studies, California Institute of Integral Studies, and Maitri Psychotherapy Institute provided me important venues to develop my thinking on many of the book's topics.

Although he died before the book got underway, I have been buoyed by the spirit of Jim Bugental, who seems to hover above my shoulder as a fierce angel, challenging me to step up, speak up and risk everything in the pursuit of truth. More than any of my Existential brethren, Jim was fascinated with the nondual deepening I was folding into psychotherapy. Given the undercover, psychedelic-journeying hippie he once was (as his wife, Liz, admitted after his death with no small glee), I know he would have loved – and himself tested – how this book extends Inward Searching into the lucency of authentic presence. In the way one loves and misses a robust competition, say of a tennis or badmitten match, or a cooperative, spirited inquiry into Truth, I miss the hearty engagement I know this book would have elicited from Jim. Among my many other Existential Therapy colleagues, members of the perennial Art of the Psychotherapist Master Group, Ernesto Spinelli, Kirk Schneider, Art Giacalone, Ado Huygens and other Daseinanalytic practitioners have been especially willing to meet me at the edge of the known and lean, to one degree or another, over that edge.

Even more so, the Lafayette sangha and on-going consultation group-turned-Dharma circle members have been steadfast in inspiring me to unpack the full arc of healing and facilitate practical access to its subtler, more dizzying reaches. A clutch of family and friend "civilians," as my partner, Nelle Engoron, speaks of non-therapists and non-Buddhists like herself, deserve credit for getting me to speak more plainly to The Mystery so elusive to speak of and to. Nelle has also been exceptionally generous in taking up any number of domestic chores I neglected for the sake of the writing; as well as in tolerating my monopolizing dinner table conversations in working out content issues foreign to her when no one else was at hand. Taken together, the encouragement, sincere questions, heartfelt confusion, patience, and at times uncompromising demand for greater clarity of the lot has unquestionably contributed to whatever merit is in these pages.

The publishing process shepherded by John Negru of Sumeru Press turned out to be one of happy collaboration. His enthusiasm for the interdisciplinary nature of the book was a welcome boost. As was his willingness to not constrict my voice by slotting the text into preconceived publishing categories. And his ready sense of humor coupled with keen editorial eye, incisive in both small and large matters yet without ever being imperious, created a fertile space for me to fine tune things, without saying either too little or too much. Whatever excesses or inadequacies remain, they have been minimized through his involvement.

The artwork of hands in the Arc of Healing montage was done by Rosiland Solomon. She was game enough to come out of the virtual medium of Photoshop and re-enter the earthy medium of pen and ink in order to render line drawings as I envisioned them.

I am additionally grateful to Padma Publishing and Richard Barron for permission to use his brilliant Longchenpa translation which ends the book. This is a no-bullshit, blessing-saturated coda of a fully realized master worthy of committing to memory. The San Francisco-based Existential Humanistic Institute has long provided me a forum for presenting the contemplative emphasis of my work to a wider audience, even as it stretches the edge of the EHI mission. My gratitude likewise extends to the London-based Society of Existential Analysis, both for hosting workshops pertaining to themes in the book and for permission to republish here what was previously published in the *Journal of Existential Analysis*. Much of the material contained in Chapter 6 appeared in two articles therein: Bradford, K. (2020). The subject matter of psychology: Psyche, Dasein, non-self. ***The Journal of Existential Analysis***, *31(2), 336-350;* and Bradford, K. (2021). Non-self Psychology: The Buddhist phenomenology of self-experience. ***The Journal of Existential Analysis***, *32(1),* 100-111.

References

Atwood, G. & Stolorow, R. (1984). *Structures of subjectivity: Explorations in psychoanalytic phenomenology*. Hillsdale, NJ: The Analytic Press.

Baraz, J. & Alexander, S. (2012). *Awakening joy: 10 steps to happiness.* Berkeley: Parallax.

Brach, T. (2003). *Radical acceptance: Embracing your life with the heart of a Buddha.* NY: Bantam.

Bradford, G. K. (1989). Tragedy and the Art of Questioning in Depth Psychotherapy. *The Humanistic Psychologist, 17*(3), 224-250.

Bradford, G. K. (2013). *The I of the Other: Mindfulness-based diagnosis and the question of sanity.* St Paul, MN: Paragon House.

Bradford, K. (2019). Radical authenticity. *The Journal of Existential Analysis, 30(1),* 113-125.

Boss, M. (1990). Anxiety, guilt and psychotherapeutic liberation. *Review of Existential Psychology and Psychiatry, 20,* 71-92.

Bugental, J. (1978). *Psychotherapy and process.* NY: Addison-Wesley.

Bugental, J. (1981). *The search for authenticity: An existential-analytic approach to psychotherapy (Enlarged edition).* NY: Irvington Publications.

Bugental, J. (1987). *The art of the psychotherapist.* NY: Norton.

Bugental, J. (1988). *The search for existential identity.* NY: Jossey-Bass. (Originally published 1976)

Dillard, A. (1974). *Pilgrim at Tinker Creek.* New York, NY: Bantam.

Ekman, P., Davidson, R. J., Ricard, M. & Wallace, B. A. (2005). Buddhist and psychological perspectives on emotions and well-being. *American Psychologist, 14(2),* 59-63.

Eschen, E. K. (2020). *Authenticity and Freedom: A Comparison of the Ideas of Ajahn Chah and James F. T. Bugental* (ProQuest No. 28088931) [Doctoral dissertation, California Institute of Integral Studies, San Francisco]. ProQuest Dissertations.

Fenner, P. (2017). *Natural awakening: An advanced guide for sharing nondual awareness.* Richmond Hill, ON: Sumeru Press.

Fisher, E. (2017). *Anxiety and the illusion of self: A phenomenological study.* Unpublished doctoral dissertation. Santa Barbara, CA: Pacific Graduate School.

Garcia, J. (2021). Dawn of the Dead. In Wenner, J. & Reich, C. (Reporters). *Rolling Stone special collector's edition: Grateful Dead.* 8-27.

Garza, E. (2018). *Getting off: One woman's journey through sex and porn addiction.* NY: Simon & Schuster.

Golas, T. (1971). *The lazy man's guide to enlightenment.* Palo Alto, CA: Seed Center.

Guenther, H. V. (Translator). (1976). Long-chen rab-byams-pa, *Kindly bent to ease us: Part 3, Wonderment, from the trilogy of finding comfort and ease.* Berkeley: Dharma.

Hafiz. (1996). *I heard God laughing.* (D. Ladinsky, Trans.). Sufism Reoriented.

Hawking, S. & Mlodinow, L. (2010). *The grand design.* NY: Bantam Books.

Heidegger, M. (1962). *Being and time.* (J. Macquarrie & E. Robinson, Trans.). NY: Harper and Row. (Original work published 1927)

Heidegger, M. (1966). *Discourse on thinking.* (J. Anderson and E. H. Freund, Trans.). NY: Harper Colophon. (Original work published 1959)

Horwitz, A. V. & Wakefield, J. C. (2007). *The loss of sadness: How psychiatry transformed normal sorrow into depressive disorder.* Oxford University Press.

Hume, D. (1978). *A treatise of human nature.* L.A. Selby-Bigge & P.H. Nidditch, (Eds.) London: Oxford University Press. (Original work published in 1739)

Husserl, E. (1962). *Ideas: General introduction to pure phenomenology.* (W. R. B. Gibson, Trans.). NY: Collier. (Original work published 1913)

Johnson, W. (2012). *Breathing through the whole body.* Rochester, VT: Inner Traditions.

Keeney, B. P. (1983). *Aesthetics of change.* N.Y.: Guilford.

Lacan, J. (1977) *Ecrits: A selection.* (A. Sheridan, Trans.) NY: Norton. (Original work published in 1966)

Laing, R. D. (1960). *The divided self.* Tavistock.

Longchen(pa) Rabjam. (2006). *The precious treasury of pith instructions.* (R. Barron, Trans.) Junction City, CA: Padma Publishing.

Loy, D. (1996). *Lack and transcendence: The problem of death and life in psychotherapy, Existentialism, and Buddhism.* NJ: Humanities Press.

Lu K'uan Yu (Luk, C.) (1970). *Ch'an and Zen teaching: First Series.* Berkeley: Shambhala.

Mahler, M., Pine, F. & Bergman, A. (1975). *The psychological birth of the human infant: Symbiosis and individuation.* NY: Basic Books.

Marcel, G. (1949). *Being and having.* (K. Farrer, Trans.). London: Dacre Press.

McLeod, K. (2001). *Wake up to your life: Discovering the Buddhist path of attention.* San Francisco: Harper.

Merleau-Ponty, M. (1962). *The phenomenology of perception.* (C. Smith, Trans.). NY: Routledge & Kegan Paul.

Merleau-Ponty, M. (1964). The child's relations with others. In, *The primacy of perception and other essays*. Ed. Edie, J. (W. Cobb, Trans). NY: Northwestern University Press. (Original work published in 1960)

Mitchell, S. (Ed.). (1989). *The enlightened heart: An anthology of sacred poetry*. NY: Harper.

Mogenson, G. (1992). Living the symptom. *The psychotherapy patient*, 8, 11-25.

Namkhai Norbu. (1986). *The crystal and the way of light: Sutra, tantra and dzogchen*. (J. Shane, Ed.). NY: Routledge.

Namkhai Norbu, C. (1994). *Buddhism and psychology*. Arcidosso, Italy: Shang Shung Edizioni.

Pattison, G. (2000). *The later Heidegger*. New York, NY: Routledge.

Rumi, J. (1995). *The essential Rumi*. (C. Barks with J. Moyne, Trans.). New York, NY: Harper.

Salzberg, S. (2004). *Loving-kindness: The revolutionary art of happiness*. Boston: Shambhala. (Originally published 1995)

Schneider, K. J. (2013). *The polarized mind: Why it's killing us and what we can do about it*. Colorado Springs, CO: University Professors Press.

Spinelli, E. (2019). What's so existential about Existential Therapy? *Existential Analysis, 30.1: 59-79.*

Strawson, G. (2016). Narrative bypassing. *Journal of Consciousness Studies, 23/1&2: 125-139.*

Thompson, M. G. (2017). *The death of desire: An existential study in sanity and madness*. London: Routledge.

Tillich, P. (1952). *The courage to be*. Yale U. Press.

Tsoknyi, R. (1998). *Carefree dignity: Discourses on training in the nature of mind*. Boudhanath, Nepal: Rangjung Yeshe Publications.

Trungpa, C. (1972). *Mudra*. Berkeley: Shambhala.

Trungpa, C. (1973). *Cutting through spiritual materialism*. Boston: Shambhala.

Trungpa, C. (1976). *The myth of freedom*. Boston: Shambhala.

Trungpa, C. (1978). *Glimpses of Abhidharma*. Boulder, CO: Prajna.

Trungpa, C. (1981). *Journey without goal: The Tantric wisdom of the Buddha*. Boulder, CO: Shambhala.

Trungpa, C. (1984). *Shambhala: The sacred path of the Buddha*. Boston: Shambhala. (Originally published 1978)

Trungpa, C. (1991). *Crazy wisdom*. (Edited by Sherab Chodzin). Boston: Shambhala.

Van Dusen, W. (1965). Invoking the actual in psychotherapy. *Journal of Individual Psychology*, 21, 66-76.

Walsh, R., & Shapiro, S. L. (2006). The meeting of meditative disciplines and Western psychology. *American Psychologist*, 61(3), 227-239.

Wegela, K. (1988). Touch and go. *Journal of Contemplative Psychotherapy*, 5, 3-23

Wegela, K. K. (2009). *The courage to be present*. Boston: Shambhala.

Welwood, J. (2000). Reflection and presence: The dialectic of awakening. In, *Toward a psychology of awakening: Buddhism, psychotherapy, and the path of personal and spiritual transformation*. Boston: Shambhala.

Whyte, D. (1992). *Fire in the earth*. Many Rivers Press.

Winnicott, D. W. (1971). *Playing and reality*. NY: Tavistock.

CPSIA information can be obtained
at www.ICGtesting.com
Printed in the USA
JSHW032004051221
20999JS00006B/17

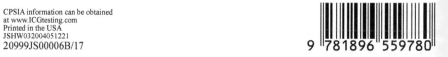